MW01514823

DEVELOPING YOUR BACKBONE

🕊

The Science of Saying NO

ANNE BROWN PHD, RNCS

www.developingyourbackbone.com

Library of Congress Control Number 2010913283

Developing Your Backbone, The Science of Saying No by Anne Brown Phd, RNCS

ISBN 1453800700/9781453800706

First printing 2010

Printed in 2010 by CreateSpace

Dedication

My clients

Acknowledgments

I owe a special acknowledgment and thanks to my teacher Dr. Fernando Flores for his profound influence on my life and my work. I am extremely grateful to all of the teachers and students in my Ontological Design Community with Dr. Flores.

It is an honor for me to thank my advisor and mentor, Dr. Ray Dorritie, whose encouragement, guidance and support from the beginning to completion enabled me to have a better understanding of the project. I am truly indebted to him for his leadership.

Love and thanks to my dear friend Suzanne Farver who's steadfast support, wisdom, laughter and encouragement assists me in crossing many finish lines including and especially this book.

Hockmeyer Studios with their (Ann, Beth, and BC) exquisite care under the guidance of my talented brother Brian deserve a very special acknowledgment and thanks!

Robyn Cruze-Harrington, a kindred book publishing spirit, who is always just a moment away, has my back, and has brought laughter and joy to this journey; thank you for your devotion to this project.

I am especially indebted to Ted Nickerson for his words of wisdom, delightful sense of humor, and for the Title.

Thank you to my blessed children Whitney and Greg who have taught me so much.

I am humbled by and grateful for the shoulders I stand on who have passed but are not forgotten: Gigi, Poppa, Aunt Roma, Dad, Mom, Charlie and Teo.

I am deeply grateful to all my close friends, clients, and family who have supported this endeavor.

Table of Contents

Authors Note

Researchers have found we are more effective in our interpersonal interactions when we are more open and aware of our blindness's. The more authentically we speak; the more successful we will be in our career, our love life, our family, and with our health and our friends. If our speaking and actions are driven by honesty, we will be in the world with authenticity, power, passion, dignity, peace and success.

People-pleasing is driven by distortion of the truth, avoidance of conflict, need to be liked, insecurity, poor self-esteem, and giving away power. Takers, addicts, bad boyfriends or girlfriends, predators, people driven by greed take advantage of people-pleasers. People-pleasers cannot take care of themselves in the presence of these people so often feel like victims in the world.

The world is smaller, more complex, and challenging. We need skills to be able to negotiate our way through the darker sides of life. I have found that implementing three distinctions I will call Backbone tools; the ability to say No with dignity, make requests, and speak authentically can radically change one's life.

All of us need Backbone Tools. When you bump up against the Bernie Madoffs of the world and they can't tolerate requests, it is time for you to move on before you find your wallet empty. The people in 12 step programs can greatly enhance their recovery by reading this book, and by being in a Backbone group learning Backbone skills. I believe for most people struggling with addiction, including eating disorders, and the friends and families of those struggling with addictions, there is a component of people-pleasing. Women who have been abused or are being abused AFTER they are in a safe environment need Backbone skills. If they learn these skills early in life they will have the tools to avoid abusive, toxic situations.

How did our obesity rate get so high? People are saying Yes to unhealthy foods that are clearly designed to line the pockets of the companies making them, not support your health. How did our addiction rates get so high? People are saying Yes to substances, which in excess have the cost of destroying our lives. We need to say No to substances, which cost us our health, our lives and support other's greed.

When we meet the unhealthy toxic people of the world we need to say No to allowing them access to us. When people try to brainwash us with lies we need to have the tools to say No to brainwashing.

The first order of business is to assess if your environment is safe. Can the people around you tolerate you becoming your own person? Can they support your truth? Again the first order of business is to assess if your environment is safe. If it isn't there are organizations, which can assist you in getting out of unsafe environments. Once you are in a safe environment start reading, get together a group, and start working. As part of your work in developing a Backbone, I also recommend you attend a Family of Origin workshop (Resources) in order to better understand your family history. We all have gifts and challenges from our families and it is important to sort these out with people trained to help us do this.

Enjoy the journey. I for one did not arrive with a strong clear voice. I, like others, am learning the joy of living powerfully with dignity and authenticity. Many of these examples are from my journey, which is ongoing. Once you are in a safe environment embrace the learning and let's get going.

Introduction

Babies are born with somewhere in the area of 100 billion brain cells. That's approximately the number of stars in the Milky Way, and, in fact, a galaxy of stars isn't such a bad way of visualizing a baby's brain, because it accurately depicts the purity and innocence of a clean but unique, individualized slate. There are no relationships, good or bad, between the stars.

Now visualize connections between the stars, like charts of constellations. That's what happens when we, as babies, are exposed to life. The nature of our experiences influences the connections between our brain cells. These connections are known as synapses, and they help us make sense of the world around us.

Initially, that world consists of our immediate family, and as children we do our damndest to make sense of it. We observe, listen, adapt and then accommodate. In dysfunctional families, however, as hard as the children of these families might try, it is impossible to accommodate everyone. [i]

In these situations, we become breeding grounds for anxiety. We try to fix everything, which, of course, is impossible, but we're determined. No, we're desperate. We overcompensate and take on traits we wouldn't have otherwise. By the time we reach adulthood, even our teen years, those traits are magnified, and the truth is now turned on its head. We say Yes when we mean No. [ii]

- Yes to sex with the ex
- Yes to paying for things we can't afford
- Yes to things we know feel good at the time and cost us our self esteem later
- Yes to numbing ourselves with food, alcohol, and drugs
- Yes to sex to be liked
- Yes to being sweet to parents and step-parents who treat us poorly
- Yes to abusive bosses
- Yes to our friends partying at our house when our parents are away
- Yes to oral sex that teenage boys want from us because we think we will be more popular
- Yes to unfair salaries

- Yes to "putting up with" and "doing more than others"
- Yes to any request from anyone because we want to avoid conflict

We wonder why we feel controlled, bullied, used and abused.

We help others, but never ask for help in return. Our Saturday plans to have fun find us doing yet another something for someone else.

Time and time again, we accept the short end of the stick. We curse ourselves for having partners who won't commit, partners to whom we're nicer and nicer, to whom we keep making sacrifices, to whom we support in their world with no reciprocation. We buy things for the relationship we can't afford, until one day our partner has moved on, found someone else. We feel used and discarded and they already have the new relationship. But we were so nice.

Or we give and give expecting our partners to do the same and when they don't we leave because we are so filled with resentment we feel entitled to leave. We gave so much and they gave so little. We keep score and we always come out giving more-the victim.

We look in the mirror and see failure-- again. Yet all we did is give and give. Resentment rears its ugly head.

Our families refuse to see our newfound success as adults and treat us like the black sheep we were growing up. They continue to manipulate us the way they did when we were the babies of the family growing up.

Our friends are addicts, and manipulate us too. How is it that we can manage a successful business but have a failed personal life?

In 30 years of practicing psychotherapy, these have been some of the stories of my patients. In every case there is a common thread: the adaptive skill of trying to please everyone. In a world that is complicated and not always friendly, people-pleasing usually has devastating results. [iii]

People-pleasers are at risk in the domains of finances, love, sex, family and friendship. How many times have you shorted yourself financially, for example, because you were unwilling to request what you deserved? How many times have you said yes to sex when you wanted to say no? How many times have you wished to walk with dignity, only to hold your head in shame or as a victim?

Warriors, by contrast, set boundaries, request what they need, and are comfortable saying *No*. The Indians in *Dances with Wolves* are excellent examples. In their world, honesty wasn't rewarded, nor was dishonesty frowned upon; instead, honest communication seemed the only form they knew.

If you haven't seen the movie, you should, as it's an epic example of two cultures clashing-that of the Sioux tribe and that of the European settlers.

The settlers slaughter Indian men, women and children with the same disregard they do animals. One scene is particularly demonstrative. It shows a traumatized buffalo calf wailing amongst a field of countless dead and skinned buffalo killed only for their hides.

By contrast, the Sioux are also portrayed hunting buffalo, and they kill as few as possible, only what they can eat and completely utilize. There is a celebration, which follows the hunt.

There was an undercurrent to everything they did that emphasized dignity. Confrontations, for example, were resolved in a way that allowed all parties to retain their dignity, even the most relatively minor ones-- like who would keep John Dunbar's lost hat.

The scene, if you recall, is a feast celebrating a successful buffalo hunt, during which Lieutenant John Dunbar, played by Kevin Costner, notices a large Sioux man has his hat:

John Dunbar: That's my hat... that's my hat!

Big Warrior: I found it on the prairie. It's mine.

Wind In His Hair: The hat belongs to the Lieutenant.

Big Warrior: He left it on the prairie. He didn't want it.

Wind In His Hair: Well, you can see he wants it now. We all know it's a soldier's hat. We all know who wears it. If you want to keep it, that's fine, but give something for it.

The Sioux warrior removes his knife and sheath from his belt and gives it to Dunbar.

Wind In His Hair: Good trade. [iv]

On the other hand, the character, Jenny, in *Forrest Gump*, is an excellent example of a people-pleaser: good, kind, nice, thoughtful, caring, sensitive—and always getting the short end of the stick.

The childhood victim of an abusive father, Jenny, the adult, has sex she doesn't want, allows men to hit her, and finally contemplates suicide. Once she acknowledges her past, however, she begins to speak authentically and finds inner peace. As one of my clients so perfectly put it after undergoing a similar transformation, Jenny "left behind her angry, defensive way of thinking."

Jenny's transformation occurs when she returns to the house in which she grew up. She and Forrest are walking along a dirt road when they approach a dilapidated, deserted house. Jenny's entire demeanor changes, and she starts throwing rocks and anything she can find at the house. One of her throws breaks a window, and Jenny falls to the ground crying. Forrest kneels down next to her.

Forrest: Sometimes I guess there just aren't enough rocks.[v]

In today's world, it's no longer optional but mandatory to learn the skills of a warrior, and there are ways to go about it which don't require we break windows, live in a teepee or join an ancient Japanese samurai sect. Today's warrior is a Life Warrior, and the process of becoming one entails learning three skills:

1. How to Say No
2. How to Make Requests[vi]
3. How to Speak Authentically[vii]

As you begin, of course, there will be fear. Fear is a normal part of change. So are awkwardness and self-doubt. Embrace them, as they signify your first steps toward becoming a warrior. No one is necessarily born with a warrior spirit, and everyone who has set out to make it a part of their lives initially might feel the same fears you will. Declare yourself a beginner, and give yourself permission to make mistakes.

If you do, you'll soon find yourself on the road to dignified and authentic living. Along the way, you may just double your income, end toxic relationships, and raise healthier children. Right from the start, you'll notice a difference. Just learning to say *No* comes with all sorts of positive change.

Endnotes

ii. Lamar, 176.

iii . Lamar, 176.

iv *Dances with Wolves,* directed by Kevin Costner. Tig Productions, 1990.

v *Forrest Gump,* directed by Robert Zemeckis. Paramount Pictures, 1994.

vi · Searle, *Speech Acts: An essay in the Philosophy of Language,*
(Cambridge:Cambridge University Press 1969), 31.

vii Harriett Rubin, " The Power of Words" *Fast Company,* no. 21 *(December* 31,
1998),

Chapter One

As anxious as you are to begin learning *How To Say No*, and as anxious as I am for you to begin to see and feel the results, let's first see what's at stake.

If people-pleasing amounted to nothing more than a series of misguided choices, we could simply add, "Correct them" to our To Do list. But that's not the case.

The consequences of people-pleasing are severe, and cost us in the domains of health, personal, finance, relationships, career, and dignity, much like any serious illness.[i]

If you learned you had cancer, you would drop everything to seek treatment. While people-pleasing doesn't carry the same stigma that the C-word does, it does come with serious consequences of its own, and requires immediate attention.

So what is this phenomenon of people-pleasing? In essence, it's the need to avoid conflict and make everyone in the world like us. It's an irrational goal that comes with all kinds of serious risks to our emotional and physical well-being.

Emotional Health Risks

Instead of engaging in healthy and relaxing conversation, people-pleasers put themselves through an emotionally-exhaustive process.

Take the following conversation:

Landlord: "You're the worst tenant I've ever had. You make too much noise. I can hear you upstairs. I can hear you in the bathroom. I can hear you on the phone.

The lights are always on. I can see them through the crack under the door. You're always washing your clothes. You're costing me a fortune."

Tenant: …

Why can't the tenant respond right away? For years he's suppressed his own ideas. The longer we play the role of people-pleaser, the less likely it is we know how we feel about anything anymore.

Instead, we revert to behavior we acquired as children, when we did our best to keep dysfunction at bay: parents yelling, hitting, drinking, bullying, intimidating, and or disappearing.

Before we respond, people-pleasers process a series of thoughts:

1. What can I say to ensure I'll be liked?
2. What is it that's troubling the other person? (This is otherwise known as mind reading.)
3. How do I phrase my response in such a way as to fend off any confrontation?

Then and only then, after having completed this exhausting mental exercise, how do we respond, with what profound and poignant words?

Tenant: Yes, you're right.

What's even more disappointing is that, in all likelihood, we actually believe it. After all, everyone in our family always told us how horrible we were. Maybe it's true.

Client: Maybe my landlord is right. Everyone in my family told me I was thoughtless, noisy, clumsy, insensitive, and a burden so it must be true. I've been trying to live quietly in her house, but I guess I'm just incapable.

Therapist: No, actually, when you pay rent to someone, you have the right to create yourself in that space. You are not horrible! This is simply a toxic environment for you.

It took some time for this client to believe he was not the bad person here. Eventually he moved out to create his own space with a gracious landlord.

If we're insecure and bullied by toxic people, the tendency is to blame ourselves. But how do we tell a toxic environment from a non-toxic one?[ii]

Setting Standards

It has to do with setting standards for ourselves and how we'll be treated. First, we have to be able to recognize when we lack such standards.

Those moments are often epiphanies, highly-charged and emotional because they're simultaneously happy and sad. They are the very sorts of memories, which, each morning, when I open the door to my office, I recall with delight.

I see myself sitting across from a client, he on one couch, I in my "chair", coffee table in between, a bowl of chocolates, water, cough drops, certificates hanging on brick walls painted white.

Client: I see what you are saying. I have never had standards for the way people can treat me.

In addition to recognizing that we don't have standards, if an environment is such that when we set standards and they are not being honored, it's toxic.

It doesn't matter what the domain: love, health, finances, community, parents, children etc. Nor does it matter whom the person. Standards are standards.

For example, many of us accept ill-mannered treatment from a doctor or lawyer because of the perceived stature of that person's job.

In fact, there's a TV commercial airing now, the likes of which I've never before seen. The scene is of a couple sitting across from each other at a restaurant, menus in hand, and a waiter approaches to take their order:

Waiter: So, do you have any questions?

Woman: What is the soup of the day?

Waiter: We have a mulligatawny soup.

Woman: Do you have any specials?

Waiter: We have a steak special today.

Woman: Oh, how is that cooked?

Waiter: its pan-seared and then…

Woman (interrupting the waiter): Does that come with a side dish? Is it grilled? Can I have it steamed? What do you recommend? What kind of pie do you have? Are you an actor? Aren't you from Ohio?

The woman won't let up. She's in an environment in which she's comfortable, and it shows. She's comfortable asking questions.

Then the scene switches to the same woman alone with her doctor in his office, sitting on his examination table. The doctor has just finished telling her the diagnosis.

Doctor: Any questions?

Woman: …

She's about to ask a question, but instead shakes her head, then waves the doctor away. Clearly, she's out of her comfort zone. The narrator takes over.

Narrator: Ask questions. Questions are the answer.

The ad is sponsored by the Agency for Healthcare Research and Quality and the U.S. Department of Health & Human Services. The point, of course, is that we shouldn't feel intimidated, nor should we feel like we're being difficult. In short, it's okay to question.

Of course, the higher our standards, the more likely it is we'll find ourselves in conflict with others. Likewise, the lower our standards, the less likely it is we'll find ourselves in conflict with others.

Yet, the need to avoid conflict is the most common thread amongst people-pleasers. You can see the conundrum.

If we lower our standards and try to please everyone, we raise the likelihood that there will be consequences:

- Lack of self-confidence
- Judgmentalism
- Anxiety
- Lack of Self-knowledge
- Physical Dangers
- Depression

Lack of Self-Confidence

People-pleasing elevates others to a place of power and fuels their self-confidence. In turn, where does that leave us?

We revert to our childhood, when we hid our needs and desires from maladaptive parents unwilling to acknowledge us as anything more than a burden, and hell-bent on compromising whatever beauties and abilities with which we may have been blessed. Our self-confidence is sapped.[iii]

In many cases, parents weren't just controlling but hurtful.

Client: Every time I told my parents what was important to me, they'd say no. I wanted to play Soccer. They made me do Debate. I wanted to be in 4H. They made me do Track. Eventually, I stopped asking. Now I'm terrified to make requests. All it does is give the other person information to hurt you with.

Therapist: No matter what damage was done to us as children, we must give ourselves permission to share our needs, desires and opinions. And we have to pick people to be in our lives who will honor those needs, desires and opinions.[iv]

Client: I have buried my needs with mental cartwheels so I could convince myself I didn't have any. It is scary, as a child to know your needs won't be met. It is even scarier to have someone hurt you with the information you gave them thinking they would take care of you. Now I'm at the point where I feel like I've risen above having any needs. I can take anything anyone can dish out and I never ask myself how I feel about what is happening.

By adulthood, people-pleasers often become arrogant about how accommodating and "nice" they are, as compared to those people who are more "difficult."

Judgmentalism

People-pleasing fuels our judgmental side. In fact, there is a direct relationship between the degree to which we people-please and the judgments we make about others.

In our desire to avoid conflict, it's easier, of course, to pass judgment than it is to confront a person or situation directly. But that's not the way of the warrior.

Imagine if the Sioux Indians had had hair salons, therapists and telephones:

Client: I hate what my hairdresser did. Look at it. I don't know what to do. The color is horrible. I look like a trollop. Actually, I do know what to do. I told everybody what a horrible job she did, and to never use her.

Therapist: What about calling the hairdresser? Hi, this is Wind in Her Hair and, well, you colored my hair the other day, and I've tried living with it, but I'm just not happy with the results. I was wondering if we could discuss ways to make it look more like what I had in mind, something less trollopy.

Hairdresser: Yes, come in this afternoon and let's talk about how to fix it.

When we go to the source of our upset, we speak authentically and honestly. Of course, in real life your hairdresser may very well tell you, "Too bad," in which case you simply don't go back.

Bad hairdresser.

You are not an awful person because you registered your upset. Remember, you can only make the request. You cannot control its outcome.

But you've got to make the request. Otherwise, you'll just build up resentment, and that, in turn, will lead to being overly judgmental.

Client: I just found out my new boyfriend can't come up with his share of the rent. I swear, this is the story of my life. Everyone I've talked to says we're moving too fast, and he's just using me. I just think about him, and I get that gnawing feeling of resentment.

Therapist: With whom do you need to have this conversation other than 'everyone'?

Client: I need to talk to my boyfriend. But what if he can't? What if he won't? What if he gets upset with me?

Therapist: Who's upset now?

Client: Me.

Therapist: So why is it standard operating procedure for you to be upset with the people you perceive to be taking advantage of you and yet you are terrified to upset them?

Client: It's like a double standard. I'll take whatever someone dishes out, but I can't handle the idea of upsetting that certain someone. What is that about?

Therapist: At the risk of sounding like a therapist, I'm going to speculate that:

1. Confrontation was scary for you as a child,
2. You're accustomed to getting the short end of the stick, and
3. The victim role is one you've not only become accustomed to but a role that actually brings a level of comfort. Let's see what will happen to you when you go to your boyfriend to let him

know how you feel. What do you think you will be able to say to him?[v]

Client: I want to work out an agreement that won't lead to me feeling resentful, so I need to figure out what it is that I want from him in the area of money and chores, things like that.

Therapist: Sounds good.

Next Week:

Client: I drew up a contract with a list of all the things he is responsible for and all the things I am responsible for. I feel great. In the past I would have let this unfairness go on forever because 'life was not fair for me as a child.' I realized a big part of my identity with people is how unfair life is for me. Drawing up this contract took ONE hour. We both agreed and we both feel great. I am starting this relationship with no resentment, which is a first. I can see where I can start to say no to my legacy of people taking advantage of me resulting in my feeling used.

Therapist: You're right. We can help you become a warrior. Have you seen the movie, *Dances with Wolves?*[vi]

Anxiety

People-pleasing creates anxiety.

Since we've only told people what we think they want to hear, there is anxiety about trying to remember what we've told everyone.

Then there is anxiety about not telling the truth, and the possibility of being found out.

And there is anxiety about ultimately hurting someone, or everyone, for that matter, if and when the truth is finally exposed.

7-year-old Julie requests of her Mom: I don't want Alison to spend the night Mom. She is so bossy. (Alison's Mom tends to look for babysitting, people pleasing Mom's.)

Julie's Mom: Ok Honey.

Alison's Mom the next day to Julie's Mom: I was so hoping Alison could spend the night with Julie at your home tonight. She has been begging me all day.

Julie's Mom: Sure, of course. At the moment Julie's Mom is trying to please Alison's Mom she actually may not remember her promise to her own daughter.

Julie, upon finding out: Mom, why can't you stand up to Alison's Mom?

Julie's Mom to herself: Good question.

Therapist's office:

Client (Julie's Mom): I made a mess and my daughter is upset with me. What can I do now?

Therapist: Take a deep breath, call Alison's Mom and say, I made a mistake. Thank you for asking about the overnight. It is not going to work for us to have Alison spend the night. (Even if Alison's Mom comes back with, "But she's made plans, what is she to do?") Then apologize to Julie.

Client: I'm starting to see how, if I don't have boundaries for myself, I can't properly care for the people I love.

Depression

The greatest tragedy that people-pleasers experience, from my perspective, is the absence of any authentic relationship with themselves. The result is an ill-defined person: a person without a strong sense of self. An example of one end of the spectrum:

When I was working as the evening charge nurse at an inpatient psychiatric unit, we admitted a woman suffering from depression. She told us horror story after horror story about how abusively her family treated her.

When we explained how visitation worked, we let her know that she could veto anyone's visitation privileges. She decided to ban her family from visiting.

To our dismay, however, we watched her become more and more depressed, to the point that she became suicidal. As bad as her family members were, without them she felt worse.[vii]

The role this patient had always played was that of the victim: "Look how poorly I'm being treated." But, as bad as it is having one's identity be that of the victim, it feels better than having no identity at all.

Lack of Self Knowledge

We require identity and self-knowledge, or at least the perception of it.

On the opposite end of the spectrum, many people-pleasers are very competent "out in the world," and are able to take on the identity of "success," in spite of the fact that they struggle to have success in their personal life.

Client: When I'm on my own at home, I feel totally ungrounded. I'm depressed. Unmotivated. When I'm at work, I've got direction.

Those around him determine this person's sense of self. When he's at work, he's one person. When he's at home, he's another.

As a child, it was the same. Outside his home, he was the best athlete, best student, great friend etc. At home, he was constantly criticized, shamed and beaten down—the black sheep of the family. He taught himself to overachieve in the world and people-please the bad guys at home! Unfortunately, he may not believe he can be successful without a toxic home.

When we do not develop our authentic selves, or if we were never given the opportunity to do so, we may also settle for toxic situations. Why? Because it's better than being alone or we believe we need them.

22

We can get by as long as there are other people around. In fact, we may even overachieve at work and in social settings. In the case of this particular client, he continued his legacy of abuse at home with one critical, cold and controlling relationship after another.

The people-pleasing, always-accommodating, victimized son became the people-pleasing, always-accommodating, victimized boyfriend, and ultimately, the people-pleasing, always-accommodating, victimized husband.

The reality is, as he continues to feed his poor self-esteem in this way, despite his highly successful career, emotionally he's more like the woman on suicide watch at the psychiatric unit.

While we can survive with nothing more than the perception of a sense of identity, in order to thrive, we require the real deal. We need to take the time to understand who we are, what we believe, what is important to us etc.

Homework

Spend time on your own to develop an inner, private life. Find a belief system bigger than yourself, like nature, religion or spirituality. Develop practices such as meditation, yoga, prayer, attending church, exercise, deep breathing, anything that grounds you.[viii]

It doesn't matter, as long as it provides a discourse that serves to ground you, and allows you to address some of life's big questions, like:

Who are you?

What do you believe?

How does the world work?

Why do bad things happen to good people?

What should you do when bad things happen to you?

When the proverbial &^%$ hits the fan, you will be ready. You will have a reserve of emotional strength. You will be grounded, a warrior ready for action.

Although many people use addictions during times of crisis, addictions do not and should not qualify as grounding practices.

On the other hand, if you believe there is something bigger than you, and if you develop practices to support your relationship to that certain something, then you never have to feel alone in the world.

Some people even prefer a spiritual base to that of a partner.

Others, however, require a partner.

Client: I have a good person in my life and I'm practicing setting healthy boundaries. The person isn't critical and cold, which is a first for me, and I'm standing up for myself, which is also a first.

Practically speaking, this relationship is premature for this person, but he felt he simply could not remain living alone, and nevertheless, he's practicing new behaviors and learning and while it's not the most ideal situation for self-improvement, it's not a detriment either.

We were able to fashion his experience with his new partner in such a way that, not only did it benefit my client, his partner was able to see individual growth in directions she was hoping to take too.

Unfortunately, sometimes the need to be with a partner trumps all, even the relationship with one's therapist. I've had clients, who, instead of leaving a bad relationship, opted to leave therapy.

Fortunately, on occasion, they return.

Client: He was married. I knew I needed to get out of being a married man's girlfriend. I just wasn't ready. I was dreading our sessions. I'd see them in my day-timer, and, instead of looking forward to them; they were nothing more than a constant reminder of what I knew I needed to do. But I wasn't ready.

Homework

Sometimes it's okay to put off change… temporarily. If you find yourself complaining about the same situation over and over, and yet you can't leave, it may not be time to leave. But it may very well be time to stop complaining. Your friends are probably tired of hearing about it.

You are choosing to stay by choosing not to leave, so ask yourself, what is the learning for me? While it doesn't sound like it, there is opportunity, even when you're stuck. Make it work for you. Sometimes you need to build your self-confidence and get your ducks in a row before you leave.

Client: I know my fears, and I get so tired of hearing myself complain: about the relationship, the drama, and my own pathetic inability to change it. I see where my stubborn loyalty keeps getting me into trouble.

I'm not blind to the abuse, and I'm not blind to the self-sabotage. It's just that staying with the familiar is less scary than braving the unknown. But now I'm ready.

Physical Dangers

Sorry to be the bearer of bad news, and sorrier still if you already knew this as a result of firsthand experience, but people-pleasers are not equipped to deal with life's darker challenges:

- Abusive relationships
- Child Molestation
- Internet Predation
- Rape
- Kidnapping

It is difficult to determine the prevalence of abuse due to definitions of and the number of places the abuse can take place e.g. families, workplace, elder care, churches, schools, child care facilities etc. but I think it is important to understand that it is far more prevalent than we would like to believe.

Some statistics of child molestation are as high as 60% of females and 45% of males are sexually abused by a family member or someone known to them and 81% of this abuse happens before puberty.[ix]

Up to 20% of children, at any given moment, are chatting with an Internet predator, which is not surprising as there are an estimated 50,000 Internet predators out there.[x]

Every five minutes a woman is raped in the United States.[xi]

Abusive Relationships

If you're already involved in a physically abusive relationship, there is no choice but to leave. If there were other choices, I would tell you. There are not.

Do not make excuses. Do not think it will stop. Do not blame yourself. LEAVE. If your abuser is under the influence of drugs and alcohol, do not rationalize. LEAVE. If he is remorseful, apologizes, and says it will never happen again, LEAVE.

It is much easier if you leave the first time the abuse happens, but better late than never. It is rare that someone who hits once will never hit again. Likewise, it is rare that someone who hits is not already being verbally and emotionally abusive.

People-pleasers are ideal prey for abusers. Who better for an abuser to seek out than the well-meaning person who:

- Wants everyone to like her
- Never stands up for herself
- Lacks self-esteem
- Transfers power away from herself each time she's engaged in conversation

Once their intuitive checklist is complete and they've set their sights on a victim, abusers know exactly how to trap their victim and keep them trapped. That's when the emotional abuse begins.

"No one would ever have you."

"I see your diet isn't working."

"You can't cook, you can't keep house, and you can't parent."

"You're lucky I put up with you. No one else would have you."

"You want too much."

"I never realized how dumb you are."

"You're the reason I didn't get the job. You embarrass me."

"You're lucky to have me."

With his victim fully questioning her own self-worth, the abuser can get away with anything.

Client: My husband is cheating on me. We're pretending to be this happy family, and I'm dying inside. I feel like I'm going crazy.

Therapist: Is this the first time?

Client: No, it's the third, at least that I know of, and each time he begged me to stay and swore it would never happen again. Now I wonder if it will ever stop.

Therapist: Why do you think you stay?

Client: I don't know.

Therapist: Does he subtly put you down saying things like:

You are so lucky to have me:

You'll never find anyone:

No one will ever put up with you:

I am the best thing that ever happened to you!

Client: How did you know? Now that you say that, he always says he is the best thing that ever happened to me and that no one will ever have me.

Therapist: You are a great offer for someone. You are bright, attractive, kind, a fabulous mother, a devoted wife, loved by the community, and you are being brainwashed to think otherwise by a subtle form of abuse.

Unfortunately, I don't know how this particular woman fared, as her husband moved the family. It's all too typical; the geographical shift. Ripe with the hope of a fresh start, the family packs up their belongings-- along with all their dysfunction-- and moves it somewhere else.

Is that it?

Are there alternative ideas to that of leaving an abusive relationship? Is it always so cut and dry? You're hit, you leave, no questions?

When I was in Bali, I interviewed a lovely, working mother and wife, and we discussed her family and values. She spoke of a family that had a strong spiritual base with daily prayer practices, authentic conversations between husband and wife, co-parenting, and mutual decision-making—overall, a family, which in my assessment, was operating with dignity.

I asked her what would happen if her husband hit her. "It depends on the circumstances," she replied instantly, "if he lost his job, or something horrible happened to someone in his family, a death etc. It would depend on what was going on."

Now, I don't support hitting and neither did she. If the behavior was an isolated incident, everyone understood the behavior was unacceptable, and her partner was willing to talk about how to better deal with his feelings, then a strong family could heal from this deviant behavior.

Child Molestation

On February 8, 2010 Oprah Winfrey interviewed 4 child molesters with their therapist on her show. I highly recommend the show for everyone and particularly for parents. Child Molesters look for vulnerable, needy children who are afraid to speak up, who need attention, and whos' parents are absent or in denial. 90% of child molesters are known to the victim and the family. Child molesters do not want a feisty, confident child who will "rat" on them. Nor do they want parents who will believe their child. The pain of having a parent who doesn't believe you if you have the courage to speak up is almost insurmountable. Heads up!!![xii]

Internet Predation

People-pleasing patterns are often established early in life, but, of course, life offers up plenty of opportunities for reinforcing those patterns. Take teen dating, for example, the greatest cost of which is the drama-based, limited discourse that accompanies "serious" dating at this young age.

Teen-dating conversations are about "hooking up", who slept with whose best friend, oral sex, lying to parents, unchaperoned parties and secret meetings, all intended to please boys in order to gain popularity with girls.

On the other hand, a better way to build self-esteem during one's teen years is to participate in activities like arts, music, sports, politics, and travel, which can teach teens about the world and develop competences.

It is also a good time to build solid friendships without sex and conversations, which revolve around sex. Teens who follow this path are better prepared and have more confidence, wisdom and seasoning when they do date.

Teens who follow this path also have a better chance of developing the self-esteem required to see through and stand up to Internet predators, who look for people with poor self-esteem, a desire to accommodate, a need for validation, and the inability to say *No*.

Internet predators know how to say all the right things, to which the typical teen response is, "Finally, someone understands me." No, it's more like, "someone is about to take advantage of you."

When young daughters grow up in very strict, rigid and highly disciplined, pious, righteous families, it can make one's teen years a challenge, to say the least.

Our teen years are tough enough. When the expectations of our parents are impossible to meet, they're that much tougher.

As teens, we want-- no, we need-- to experiment, try new things, and test out our ideas on life. We need a strong and flexible family environment that allows for some playing room.

When our family doesn't understand the importance of some latitude, one of two things will often result:

1. We rebel.
2. We become compliant. (And what is compliance if not a form of people-pleasing?)

Neither is desirable, and each comes with consequences. Enter the Internet predator.

The Internet predator can make mincemeat of either type of teen, the rebel or the people-pleaser. For the rebel, the predator provides a means for acting out. Of course, unbeknownst to the teen, the predator is just as controlling as her family.

As for the people-pleaser, the predator is just another person to whom she doesn't have the backbone to say No. What's more, as we've seen, people-pleasers, by default, transfer power whenever they engage in conversation.

All this makes for an easy feast for the predator, who, after some seductive talking, proposes an opportunity to meet, and the rest, of course, becomes material for news anchors and statisticians.

The seduction, it should be pointed out, can take almost any form. It doesn't always have to be a male predator appealing to a rebellious teen, for instance.

We know only too well the story of the 13-year old girl who committed suicide as a result of the predacious Mom down the street who was bullying her on the Internet.

Homework

How were you raised? How are you raising your children now? If we don't do some work on ourselves, we are destined to recreate history. Attend a Family of Origin Workshop (Resources) to better understand your history.

As children introduced to the darker side of humanity, we cannot help but try to find a way to cope, and it is imperative that, as adults, we develop an understanding of:

1. What we had to cope with growing up,
2. What behaviors we adopted in order to cope, and
3. What new tools we need to negotiate our way through life.

More times than not, in my practice, clients developed people-pleasing as a coping mechanism, and the tools with which they went on to successfully negotiate through life were those of the warrior, the abilities to: Say No, Make Requests, and Speak Authentically.

Kidnapping and Rape

The feminist theory of rape is male dominance over women, abusive power over women, and an act of power to dominate women. In this country we women have legal rights, which protect us from physical dominance. Having the presence, energy, mindset of a warrior is no guarantee you will not be raped AND it is counter to the victim mentality of being dominated by a male.[xiii]

Kidnappers, too, are more prone to release someone who makes their life miserable by fighting back.

I learned the hard way that we cannot always count on our bodies to react in ways that will protect us if and when we are threatened. I unconsciously chose checking out and amnesia when I was mugged years ago.

On the other hand, a friend of mine who was accosted in a parking garage grabbed her umbrella, growled ferociously, and went after her attacker who fled.

Having warrior energy is not a guarantee you won't be the victim of a crime. However, a strong body that carries itself with dignity combined with strong conversations that support our dignity can have a powerful presence in the world.

Takers

People-pleasers aren't only at risk from predators. Takers of any sort seek out people-pleaser profiles.

Addicts, for example, are the quintessential takers, and they can "smell" people-pleasers the way sharks can smell a drop of blood: from a mile away. Often times, however, those addicts are closer to home. In fact, typically they are people we love and care about deeply.

It has been particularly noteworthy in my practice just how many clients-- with whom I've worked on overcoming people-pleasing-- have addicts in their lives. It's noteworthy but not surprising.

We've all heard of Tough Love, and it is, in fact, one of the recommended ways to help addicts. People-pleasers, however, have a challenging time with the "tough" part of tough love, and, as a result, serve only to enable the addict's behavior.

The parents of one very tough-to-treat addict wrestled with this concept continually. On occasion, the husband would send his lovely wife in to confess his latest sin e.g. new car for the poorly recovering addict, increase in allowance for the poorly recovering addict etc. In spite of the family slips: the addict with her addiction, and the parents with their enabling, they now have healthier relationships as they walk down the path of a family in recovery. What they lacked in "tough" they more than made up for with love, perseverance, detachment, family, unity, loyalty and belief!

Another mother, that of a young man from a wealthy family facing his 12th DUI, paused and required a moment of contemplation when I asked her this question:

"When your son gets his 13th DUI, can the family NOT send lawyers to get him off the charges?

"No, "she said, " someone will call his lawyer to get him out of trouble."

"He knows that so there is no reason to stop drinking," I replied.

The road for both the addict and the enabler is long and bumpy.

It's a bitter irony that the person who only wants to avoid conflict—the people-pleaser—can do so much damage to those she loves the most. It's not just the addicts in her life who are put at increased risk; it's her spouse, children, and friends too.

Our Relationships

Client: I want to divorce my husband. He's cold. He doesn't talk to me. All he does is work, and if he's not working, he's playing golf. The kids are not close to him-- he's so strict.

Therapist: Have you brought these concerns up with your husband?

Client: Oh no, I could never do that.

Therapist: There will be no divorce under this roof until you start talking to your husband. You need to learn to speak up, and he needs to be able to fight for his marriage.

One of the most damaging emotional traumas is to deprive one's partner the right to fight for his marriage.

When we tell our spouse only what we think he wants to hear, when we are always nice and accommodating, we build up a long list of secret complaints and resentments, and that's a recipe for disaster.

One partner thinks everything is fine, and the other is on her way to divorce. The same phenomenon occurs in dating.

Almost all of us are guilty of becoming chameleons when we date. We forget everything that made us successful in other aspects of our life.

Some of us, however, take it to more of an extreme than others.

Client: I'm in debt… bad. I can't keep up with his lifestyle. My new boyfriend wants me with him all the time at all of his functions. I don't have the clothes for all of these fancy functions so I go out and buy them with money I don't have. I'll never wear these outfits if I am not with him. Now I have debt on my credit cards. I have never spent money I don't have. I don't know how I am going to pay off my credit cards. I am thousands of dollars in debt.

Therapist: How about, when the next invitation comes, if you say, I would love to go, but I don't think I have the clothes necessary for that event.

I really enjoy being with you and doing these things with you, but I've been spending money I don't have for other events we've gone to together.

Debt is something I have never allowed to happen to me. I've never spent what I don't have. I'm really uncomfortable and scared, actually. I need to change my ways. I hope you understand.

I have had clients who regretted taking too much time off work to travel with men, and others who gave up good jobs without first discussing how money was going to flow in the new marriage.

We can't simply join "his world" willingly, without requiring him to do the same of ours. Otherwise, at best, we're left resentful. At worst, we're left resentful and broke.

Client: I go to every one of his boring events, yet he hasn't met a single one of my friends. I spend time with his kids; yet I can feel them hating me, feel them almost calculating how much I'm costing them of their inheritance. Do you realize he won't go to my parents' 30th wedding anniversary? My whole family is going to be there. I am so angry I don't know what to do.

Therapist: How about if you say, I'm not going to be able to attend this function or that function with you. Your children have expressed a desire to have some alone time with you so I will honor that request.

I'm really going to miss you at my family's gathering. Everyone's asking about you, and they were all hoping this would be their opportunity to meet you. I hope you will join me with my family soon.

We have to take care of ourselves, and when things get lopsided, it makes it that much more difficult. In order that things don't get lopsided, we must have a voice in our relationships.

Client: I feel like I'm begging when I ask my husband for money. I can't stand it. I have always made my own money and never had to ask anyone to take care of me.

Therapist: Tell him you have an important and potentially difficult conversation you would like to have, and ask him to pick a time that is mutually convenient.

Begin by telling him you made a mistake by not having this conversation sooner (bad business decision on your part). Give him a short synopsis of your relationship with money, particularly as it relates to your recent past and your career.

Be open to hearing his history with women and money. Be clear what you are asking for. If he asks you what you would need to be happy, give him the amount. Don't say, 'I don't know, what do you think?'

Be clear on what you need in order not to build resentment. Discuss, take a break, discuss. Talk to those in your circle of trusted friends (other adults who may have worked this out, not rabble-rousers).

Keep the discussion going until neither party has resentment, keeping in mind that men are more inclined to try to solve problems than they are to express the empathy and compassion you might have received from your female friends.

Just give him the breakdown, and let him solve it. If it's a different solution than what you had in mind, you can either accept or decline.

Homework

When, and under what circumstances, have you been a chameleon?

If doing things "his way" is the only way, then it is time to assess the situation, not ignore it, as that can only lead to further resentment.

If our requests are declined time after time, then at some point we have to admit to ourselves that we're not really involved in an equitable relationship at all.

Ask yourself what type of relationship you want, not what type of relationship you think you're a good enough person to ever find or what type of relationship he tells you you're not good enough to find.

While it's important to take care of ourselves in all domains, it's particularly important to take care of ourselves in the domain of finances. It's one thing to heal a broken heart, quite another to heal a broken heart along with a broken wallet.

Resentment kills passion, so it is not uncommon for people-pleaser to have affairs. The people-pleaser feels justified, because "look at all the injustices my partner has committed." WRONG.

Client: I have a wonderful man in my life. He's warm, funny. He adores me. He listens to me. He cares what I'm doing, how I'm doing, and—you know what—I deserve him. He's the exact opposite of my husband. What do I do?

Therapist: Close one door before you open another. If you want warm and fuzzy, request it of your husband. If you still don't get it, require it. Yell, scream, do whatever you need to do to get his attention, but get it.

Drag his cute, little, cold self into therapy, and see if he can deliver what you think you want. Ask! Ask for what you need!

How many people leave their marriage for the next person, only to leave the next person because they did not really know him? How many families have been traumatized because someone had an affair, only to leave the affair?

Close one door before you open another, and make sure you actually hear the door shut behind you.

It is our job in a partnership to have the courage to bring up our concerns, to give our partner the opportunity to address those concerns and fight for his marriage. Ending a marriage in which one person has not had the chance to fight to keep it produces suffering that can take years to get over.

The Children

Then there are the children of the divorced family. The children, of course, no longer have full access to both parents all the time. What if

Dad forgets about me? What if Mom forgets about me? What about new spouses and new children coming on the scene?

Fearing abandonment, what do you think children do, particularly daughters? You guessed it. They take on people-pleasing skills.

Abandonment is a very real concern for children of divorce. Researchers have found those children, especially daughters, are more worried about losing Dad, and sometimes Dad uses this fear for manipulative purposes. He does so for a variety of unhealthy reasons, sometimes unconsciously, sometimes not.[xiv]

Client: My parents are divorced, and my dad lost his job. I think I should cancel my summer plans and go live with him, give him some support, and make sure he is looking for a new job.

Therapist: Actually, given that you are 18 and your dad is 45, I think you are both adults and it is not your responsibility. Dad probably has his network of support, as do you, and he can rely on them. It's a nice thought, but I don't think it makes sense for you to be the mom, making sure he does what he is supposed to do.

It takes an emotionally-healthy parent to reassure children during divorce. Both parents need to provide a stable, predictable, consistent, loving environment for their children to move forward and become autonomous, authentic young adults. Unfortunately, that is not always the case.

Client: I'm worried about going away to college. My mom recently went through a divorce and is alone. I am the oldest son and I think I should stay home and help her.

Therapist: I'm sorry your Mom and your family went through a divorce, though she is not your responsibility. It is in your mom's best interest for you to get back to normal as soon as possible. That means going to the school of your dreams. You can be in closer contact than you might otherwise have been, but, really, what Mom needs is to find other people going through what she is going through, and develop her own network of support.

Blame

When divorce breaks up a family, children often assign blame to Mom, no matter whether Dad was a womanizer, had an affair, or was an absentee dad and husband.

So many fabulous women I've worked with feel that their children, particularly their daughters, blame them for failed marriages.

It's not just the kids who are likely to feel this way. It's society in general that tends to feel it is the woman's job to keep the marriage together.

It takes emotionally healthy parents to address this issue responsibly, otherwise dysfunctional patterns can and will present themselves in their children.

In some cases, one parent is the "stronger" parent, and he or she "protects" the children from the unpleasant aspects of the "weaker" parent. In other cases, the parents are stronger as a couple than as two separate individuals.

In either case, unfortunately, when divorce occurs, the strong part of the parental bond, however it may have manifested itself, usually disappears. The children, at a time of major crisis, are left to deal with two separate individuals and all their foibles.[xv]

People-Pleasing Parents

Of course, if one of the parents is a people-pleaser, the results can be devastating. I've seen it happen before the first child is even born.

Client: All these people are coming to watch the birth of our first child. They're expecting to be in the birthing room with me, and I'm starting to panic. I don't know if I want so many people around, but my husband is putting pressure on me to be nice to everyone. After all, it's everyone's first grandchild.

Therapist: What do you want?

Client: I don't know. He's right. It is everyone's first grandchild, and my husband just wants to please the families. Who am I to take away that experience for the grandparents?

Therapist: The child's mother.

Client: Oh!

Therapist: Let's talk first about how you, and then your husband, want to welcome your first child. If you're unhappy with your environment, that will translate to your child. Mom and unborn child are the two most important people to be supported at the time of the birth.

How about saying to your husband, Honey, I'd like us to be alone for the birth of our first child. Everyone can be in the waiting room. I am just not comfortable with an audience, and then your husband can say; we have decided it will just be the two of us in the delivery room, and, once our child is born, the grandparents can rotate in. Thanks for understanding.

Homework

Can you begin to see how people-pleasers cannot properly take care of others? Think back to the story of Julie's mom, too. Think about where you have not been able to take care of those you love because of your inability to say No, your need to avoid conflict, or your inability to make requests.

People-pleasers think they can take care of the addicts in their lives, and they think they can take care of their children, but what addicts, children and other dependents need are boundaries and someone who can enforce those boundaries.

Simply put, if we can't take care of ourselves, we cannot take care of others.

One of the best examples of what happens to children with people-pleasing moms comes courtesy of the least likely of all places: the crude, Comedy Central cartoon sitcom called South Park.

If you've ever seen it, Cartman, of course, is the obese, spoiled, bigoted, heartless brat everyone loves to hate. And Cartman's mom is the town slut-- not only is she unable to say *No* to her son, she is unable to say *No* to any of the men in the whole town of South Park, Colorado.

It's funny, unless Cartman's behavior happens to mimic that of our own children. Children will act out and continue to act out until we stop trying to please them. It isn't our job to give them everything they ask for, which is exactly what Cartman's mom does. Instead, it is our job to love, guide, and discipline with confidence.

Beyond the Family

Moms are not the only people who must learn to say *No* to their children. The results of people-pleasing extend well beyond the individual and her family. Their impact is seen and felt in communities worldwide.

When schools don't stand up to bullies, for example, the entire student body feels the consequences. Students don't have a safe environment in which to learn, and the victims have negative lifelong consequences.

When U.S. regulatory agencies fail to enforce financial institutions rules and regulations, the effects are pervasive. The current economic crisis cost hundreds of thousands their jobs and savings, not just here at home, but around the world.

When churches don't discharge sexually abusive priests, entire belief systems are compromised, and the victims suffer lifelong consequences.

In the world today, it's imperative to have the backbone to say No.

In the Northeast community where I worked some time ago, when drug dealers moved into the Projects, all the mothers banned together to report the dealers who were then kicked out and/or arrested. This is an example of women banding together and producing a power greater than one. We can all learn from this courage.

The movie, *Pray the Devil Back to Hell*, chronicles thousands of women who banded together to end the civil war in Liberia.[xvi] These were otherwise ordinary women of all ages who took on warlords in order to restore peace to their war-ravaged homeland. All wore white t-shirts on the back of which six simple words were written, We Want Peace. No More War.

But those few words represented so much of what we're talking about:

1. The ability to say No,
2. The ability to make requests, and
3. The ability to speak authentically.

These women risked their lives, as we can't forget that there are many countries in which women don't have the same rights we do. We have all watched with horror how the Taliban treat women.

"The people who did this to me don't want women to be educated. They want us to be stupid things," reported Shamsia Husseini, one of 11 Afghan girls who returned to class after being attacked with acid two months prior. [xvii]Take note that this young woman is saying No in a very dangerous situation.

Remember the young Afghan Olympian who said her brother would kill her for competing in the 2000 Summer Games?

The reformist movement in Iran marching and chanting "Death to the Dictator" taking a stand for justice and freedom!

Viewed from this perspective, it's almost our patriotic duty as women to be the independent thinkers and doers that our laws have evolved to allow us to be. If we don't, what message are we sending the women of Liberia, Afghanistan and others around the world?

It's our worldly duty to speak up. The informant who alerted police to the terrorist plot planned for Heathrow Airport in London had the backbone to say, "No, I don't think so."

And, of course, on September 11, 2001 the forty passengers and crewmembers of Flight 93, armed with nothing more than courage, stood up and said No to the hijacking terrorists.

We can't help but remember with tears Todd Beamers words, "Let's roll," as they changed destiny by changing the direction of the plane, which crashed in a field just outside Shanksville, Pennsylvania not into the Pentagon.

Jasper Schuringo who with the help of others on Northwest flight 253 stopped Umar Farouk Abdulmutallab from blowing up the aircraft en route from Copenhagen to Detroit.

Find a hero for yourself. Find someone whose courage to say No gets your juices going! Put this hero on your wall, in your wallet, anywhere and everywhere. Jump on the train of dignity beginning with the ability to say No to all the toxicity, negativity, and insecurities that stand in the way!

Heard enough? Ready to learn how to say *No*?

Me too. Let's get started.

Endnotes

---

[i] Harry Levinson, *The Great Jackass Fallacy.* (Cambridge: Harvard University Press, 1973), 36.
caca

[iii] Levinson, *The Great Jackass Fallacy,* 39-40.

[iv] Claire Raines and Lara Ewing, *The Art of connecting: How to Overcome Differences, Build Rapport, and Communicate Effectively with Anyone* (New York: Amacon, 2006), 111-115.

[v] Seth Allcorn, *Codependency in the Workplace: A Guide for Employee Assistance and Human Resource Professionals.* (New York: Quorum Books, 1992), 14.

[vi] *Dances with Wolves,* directed by Kevin Costner. Tig Productions, 1990.

[vii] W.S.F. Pickering and Geoffrey Walford, *Durkheim's Suicide: A Century of Research and Debate* (United Kingdom: Routledge, 2000), 11-20.

[viii] Mary Anne La Torre, " Meditation and Psychotherapy: An Effective Combination," *Perspectives in Psychiatric Care* 37 no.3 (2001): 103.

[ix] Christiane Sanderson, *Counseling Adult Survivors of Child Sexual Abuse.* (London: Jessica Kingsley, 2006), 27.

[x] Benjamin Radford, "Predator Panic: A Closer Look," *Skeptical Inquirer* 30, no. 5 (September 2006): 20.

[xi] Lynn Norment, "What's Behind the Dramatic Rise in Rapes?" *Ebony* 46, no. 11 (September 1991): 92.

[xii] *The Oprah Winfrey Show,* February 08, 2010.

[xiii] Ann J. Cahill, *Rethinking Rape* (New York: Cornell University Press, 2001), 19.

[xivxiv] Judith S. Wallerstein and Joan B. Kelly, *Surviving the Breakup: How Children and Parents Cope with Divorce* (New York: Basic Books, 1966), 55-75.

[xv] Wallerstein, *Surviving the Breakup: How Children and Parents Cope with Divorce,* 77.

[xvi] *Pray the Devil Back to Hell* directed by Abigail E. Disney and Gini Reticker, Fork Films, 2008.

[xvii] "Verbatim", *Time* (February 2, 2009): 20.

Chapter Two

Simple or Not?

On the surface, it appears to be a pretty simple proposition: Just say No!

Sometimes it is simple:

"Want to go for a hike?"

"Should we have the Mansons over for dinner?"

"How about some of Mom's meatloaf?"

Sometimes it's not, though-- for example, as we negotiate our way through life:

"Would you like to go out with me Saturday night?"

"Can I borrow $50? It would really help me out."

"Would you mind watching my kids after school?"

And sometimes it's impossible, for example, if you're in an abusive relationship and at risk of injury.

But the majority of the time, it's okay to say No, so let's define exactly what we're talking about. When it comes to Saying No, it's often easier to discuss what it's not about.

Saying No is not about providing excuses.

For example, my friend's 16-year old daughter has epilepsy. She loves her time at home with her family, and often doesn't want to go out with her friends. At the same time, she doesn't want to hurt her friends' feelings. Her dad's advice to his daughter was to "play the epilepsy card."

"There are plenty of times," Dad told his daughter, "that epilepsy doesn't work in your favor. You might as well work it to your advantage when you can. Just tell your friends you've been having seizures and you aren't feeling up to it."

While Dad's advice is well-intentioned, it is detrimental. In essence, it's teaching his daughter people-pleasing behavior and habits. Specifically, it's teaching her:

1. To feel guilty about saying No,

2. It's bad to have and express true feelings, and

3. There is something about her that isn't normal and is "less than" as opposed to the idea that there's something about everyone that isn't "normal," that everyone has some "thing" in their life and that is what makes us unique.

If you think about the excuses you use, they almost always make you a victim. Illness is an overused story for not wanting to do something.

"I don't feel well."

"I'm tired."

"I didn't sleep well."

Even if and when any of these are true, there's no reason to mention them. Warriors say No with dignity, not with excuses.

"No, I can't do that. Thanks for asking. I hope you'll ask me again."

Saying No is not a Rejection.

If I ask you to get me a cup of tea and you say No, your answer has nothing to do with me or whether you like me. No is not a reflection of your emotions. It is an answer to a question. If we can truly internalize this interpretation, our lives will become so much easier.

I remember a conversation I had with a salesman regarding the annual renewal of some advertising. When I gave him my final decision to cut my advertising in half for the coming year, he said, "You're doing this because you don't like me!"

At this point I had known this person for 15 minutes. I was expanding my advertising into different areas. Those two statements were facts. I made my decision based on diversifying my advertising, not on my like or dislike of this person.

I had a similar experience with a car salesman. This one refused to allow me to decline. In our conversation regarding price he said, "If I ask my manager to go to this low price, you have to accept the offer. I can't ask him if you won't buy the car at this price." I walked out and found a salesman at a different dealership that was free to negotiate until we were both satisfied.

Unfortunately, I believe many of us are trapped in the interpretation that saying No is a rejection. If it hurts me to hear No, it must hurt you, so I will protect all of us: I won't say No to you, and I won't ask questions in a way that you can say No to me.

Where's the dignity in that?

People-pleasers expend a great deal of energy during conversation trying to avoid confrontation. We formulate questions and statements designed in such a way as to avoid use of the word, No, as opposed to formulating questions and statements which best express our true feelings.

How can we walk with dignity if we can't speak with integrity? How can we have self-knowledge if we spend more time formulating thoughts, statements and responses that don't represent our true feelings than those that do?

Saying No is not about Controlling Outcomes.

When we say No, it doesn't mean we're control freaks. Saying No is simply an expression of what we can or cannot do.

If we don't like the pre-nup, for example, it doesn't mean we're being unreasonable. It means there are aspects of it we simply don't like.

It becomes important, however, that we have the ability to express what it is we like and dislike. If all we have is the ability or courage to say, "I don't like it," then—even if we don't intend to-- we might very well come across sounding like control freaks, even to ourselves.

On the other hand, if we:

1. Set standards for ourselves, and
2. Develop the ability to clearly state why we don't feel our standards are being met, and then it's clear to everyone that we're simply dignified in our ways, not controlling.

What happens when people sign pre-nups with which they're uncomfortable?

They begin the marriage with resentment, and, slowly but surely, chip away at it like they're felling a redwood with a hand axe.

Homework

Some of us are better at articulating our thoughts than others. If you struggle with words, the best way to get better is the same way you would approach any activity in which you wanted to improve your skills: Practice.

You can practice in front of the mirror, or you can practice with a partner.

Saying No does not Mean we're Difficult.

When we say No, it does not mean we're being a pain in the ass. Once again, it is simply an expression of what we can or cannot do.

And what we can or cannot do relates directly to the standards we set for ourselves. It doesn't relate at all to the way we may feel about one person or another.

But that's one of the worst fears of the people-pleaser, that someone will think we don't like them. So there's this constant paranoia that we're being difficult or a pain in the ass.

Homework

What you call being difficult I call being differentiated. I want you to have opinions and standards for how people can or cannot treat you.

People-pleasers want to fit in and not be noticed. However, this precludes you from having an opinion that is different from what you perceive others' opinions to be.

If it helps you to get a little bolder, practice pretending you are in a contest to be the best warrior. People-pleasers don't make good warriors, but we all need a bit of warrior that we can store away in reserve for use at the right time.

Stop your addiction to being nice! Find another adjective to aspire to, such as: alive, passionate, colorful, exciting, or unpredictable.

Client: My boyfriend of a year is not sure if I am the one. He wants to see other women before he closes the deal with me. I'm so afraid I might lose him. I feel that I should go along with his request. What should I do? It breaks my heart to think of him with another woman, but I think I have to do this. I actually think he is bored with me.

Therapist: Well, lets get bored off the table. This may be the hardest and best move you have ever taken in the domain of love.

The adult men I see in my office tell me they like a woman who requires them to be the best they can be. How about if you say, Great idea, let's shake things up a bit. We will both see other people, and not each other. If I am still available after you have checked out your other options, we can talk. If not, it was nice spending time with you. I know I am a great offer for someone, and if you are not that someone, there's no reason to drag this thing out if it's not going anywhere.

Client: Wow, I don't think he meant that we wouldn't see each other. I think he wants to have his cake and eat it too.

Therapist: Do you want that?

Client: I think if I agree to it, I will be so insecure and needy I will be a drag to date anyway.

Therapist: The right relationship is the one in which you are eager to be the best you can be. You are telling me his offer is going to facilitate you being insecure, needy and clingy. Is that what you want?

Client: No, I actually feel energized just by the idea of taking a stand for what a great offer I am, and saying No to the BS he was trying to sell me on.

Therapist: Ahh, a nice bit of the warrior lady is being born.

Speak up!

Here's an ironic twist: a therapist trying to bully his client, who also happened to be my client!

My client was in couple's therapy with his wife. The therapist was pushing hard for a desired outcome for the couple, and the man had to continually remind the therapist each week of feelings he'd expressed in previous sessions.

Client: Every week my wife and I attend therapy, I feel as though everything I had to say the week before has been discounted. We begin the session as though we're working on this viable marriage, whereas I explained the week before that they did not have my buy-in to a viable marriage.

Therapist: How about if you begin the session with a recap of what you said and Let's start from here.

In a similar situation, another client going through a tough divorce had a lawyer she didn't trust.

Client: Every time I see my lawyer, he tells me what I can't get and how I should go easy on my husband. I don't trust that he's best representing me-- my husband, maybe, but not me!

Therapist: Have you told him how you feel?

Client: No, I'm afraid I might upset him, and I need him now.

Therapist: Actually, you need someone you can trust, even if you have to start over entirely. Both parties in a divorce need to be able to negotiate to the point that, when all is said and done, both feel they have had a chance to take a stand for what they believe is fair and just. Otherwise, there's resentment.

I recommend you have a conversation with your lawyer about how you feel. If he doesn't do what you need him to do, think long and hard about what next steps you should take that are in YOUR best interest.

Ultimately, the client hired a new lawyer, who she finally felt was "on her team." It was a minor inconvenience but well worth the interruption, and thank goodness she did. Later, we discovered that the first lawyer had been through his own divorce just prior to taking on my client's case. Objectivity might not have been his strongest suit at this time.

Mind Reading

Client: I am so angry with my wife, I feel like I don't even like her.

Therapist: Have you told her what's bothering you?

Client: No, it's hard for me, and I think she ought to know anyway. I would know what I was doing wrong if she was upset.

Therapist: Really. Where did you get your degree in mindreading? I have been in this business of the mind a long time, and I don't read minds. What makes you think you can?

Client: First, she didn't give me what I wanted on my birthday, and she should know what I want. I could tell you what she wants at any given moment.

She hasn't cooked my favorite meal in weeks. It's linguine with clams, and she used to cook it once a week. She would always leave a love note in my lunch box, and she hasn't done that in a long time. She just isn't taking care of me the way I think she should.

Therapist: What is going on in your wife's life?

Client: Well, we have a new baby, who takes a lot of my wife's time, but she isn't working. I am carrying us financially.

Therapist: What do you think your wife needs at this time?

Client: Well, she has always wanted a baby so I think she probably has everything she wants.

Therapist: Well if you haven't asked her what she needs during such a life changing event you just failed Mind Reading 101. Let's try a new way of being in your marriage. You will say No to mind reading and yes to conversations. Speak up.

The Second Time Around

Client: My new wife and I fight about only one thing. She feels I spoil my children from my first marriage. I actually do give them everything they ask for, so she is probably right. But their mom is a drug addict, and when I was younger, I was a workaholic and never around.

Therapist: Do you think your kids know this about you? Let me put it another way, do you think your kids are working you, because they know you feel guilty?

Client: I never did, but my new wife absolutely thinks that is the case.

Therapist: How is this really helping you, or anyone, for that matter?

Client: I feel like I'm there for them now.

Therapist: Did your father give you everything you asked for? Should any parent give any child everything they ask for?[i]

Client: Probably not. But I feel so guilty.

Homework

Is this you? Feeling guilty about anything accomplishes nothing.

Take responsibility for your actions by having conversations about what you feel so guilty about. Speak up! Ask to have a conversation with all of your children. Bring up the past, and ask each and every one of your children how your behavior affected them in their lives.

Were you absent most of the time?

Were you high most of the time?

Were you broke? Sad? Short-tempered?

Dad: I think I might have been overly consumed with building my business at the expense of you kids and the family. What do you think?

Allow each child to talk about his or her experience. Listen for blame, pain, sadness and anger, and discuss everyone's emotions.

Allow your children their illusions, their magical thinking, their experience of what happened, apologize for your part, and continue the conversations until the experiences can be filed under "Resolved." Whatever the issue, handle it this way.[ii]

If you never do this, you will raise spoiled children. What's more, they will still carry their pain and unresolved issues.

If no one, particularly our parents, ever talked to us directly about real issues, then it's unlikely we will think to do it ourselves. But we must.

If you're afraid—if you allow your children to bring up their issues— they might not like you, you are literally blackmailing yourself, to the point that you will never say No to your children. Everyone loses in that scenario.

Not from a material perspective, of course, but in terms of thoughtless, insensitive, hurtful actions of the past, those things will forever remain unresolved.

You need to be able to say No to anyone and everyone, but especially to your children.

You also need to be accountable for your actions with everyone, but especially your children.

These breakdowns are more common than you think. Many people refuse to stop spoiling their children and, in so doing, cause substantial damage to their marriages and their children.

People-pleasing Symptoms

If you are scared to speak up, or if-- when you say No-- you:

1. Accompany it with an excuse
2. Feel like you are rejecting someone
3. Feel like you are a control freak
4. Feel like you are being difficult
5. Feel like you are going to cause conflict

Then it's very likely you are engaged in some form of people-pleasing.

There are other symptoms, too, which are less easy to self-identify without some explanation:

- Overachievement accompanied by low self-esteem[iii]
- Adherence to mainstream thinking
- Mistaking drama for excitement

People-pleasing is a deep crevasse to climb out of, no question, because the causes are deep-rooted, but we've been through worse, right?

Overachievement Accompanied by Low Self-esteem

One client, who showered and washed her hair for our first session (which was over the phone!), had bloody knuckles by the time she made it out of the crevasse.

When she heard her husband pull up in the driveway, she would hang up. She hid payment for our sessions from her husband too. We weren't able to meet in person until years later.

She had a history of abandonment, loss and neglect. One parent died when she was young and the other parent turned to alcohol to deal with the pain. As many children do in these and similar situations, my client stepped up to take care of the surviving parent and raise her siblings.

And, as an adult, she did what many adults who have walked in her shoes do. She recreated her history, attracting people in her personal life that delivered abandonment, loss and neglect. She responded as she had as a child, by overachieving.

In fact, the worse the situation, the stronger she felt. She could handle anything! The abandonment, loss and neglect fed her poor self-esteem and insecurities, while the overachieving fueled her lack of standards for the way people could treat her and her arrogance about how much she could handle.

She relished that she was so strong yet not a complainer. In her mind, complaining about toxicity and abuse was weak. She was the quintessential, people-pleasing overachiever with little self-esteem.

Client: I'm a bad wife. I have ADD, and don't know how to run a house. There are boxes, piles and messes everywhere. I can't finish anything. I hoard all my possessions from my childhood. My husband's doctor says there's something seriously wrong with me. I have seven children, who seem to be doing really well. I'm not sure how, but they are.

Therapist: Can you see that you alternate from handling more in a day than most of us do in a lifetime to feeling worthless? One minute you report handling monumental challenges; the next minute, you can't find anything redeeming about yourself, and are inclined to believe anyone who decides to vomit on you. Neither interpretation is accurate and you need emotional boundaries.

Client: I know I'm a good person. I have more love and kindness than most people I know. People who really know me say I'm the most beautiful person they know.

Therapist: When you describe how people who love you speak about you, you are closer to where you want to be. You need to develop standards for how you will allow people to treat you, and standards for the sort of environments in which you will allow yourself to be.

It takes strength to require people to respect you. Your definition of strong is, I can handle all the toxic environments I find myself in. That is not strong to me. That is being a victim.

It takes strength to push back on people who want to vomit on you. Real strength is requiring people to respect you and treat you well.

Once you take a stand against the bullshit in your life, the loving person that's inside you will be more authentic. If the loving person is nothing more than a symptom of people-pleasing, it isn't real.

To better understand this concept, rent the movie, *Pray the Devil Back to Hell.* [iv] The Liberian women became warriors when they had to. When they disbanded their organization, they disbanded it with the powerful words, 'we will be back if the fighting comes back. We will be back if our children/country need us to come back.' All of us need warrior energy.

Strength is not what you can handle. Survival is what you can handle.

Strength is having the courage to say No to toxic people and places.

But it's difficult to recognize and accept how toxic our worlds are. We get caught up in the idea that we are the nice people, and the people with standards are the difficult ones.

Sometimes we gain weight, shut down, or become numb rather than feel the pain of the toxicity we have allowed ourselves to believe is acceptable. Do you do any of these things?

The conversation I shared with you is one the client and I had had countless times. It took some time for her to get to that point.

That said, there were major turning points, and one of the biggest was when she shifted her definition of what strong was. It was at that point that she climbed on the fast track to functional health. The point at which I knew we'd arrived was when she started biting off life as fast as she could: enrolling in school, getting out in the community, commitment to self-care etc.

When we feel the need to make up for lost time, it's a signal that we're on our way to warriorhood.

Mainstream Thinking

When we fall asleep at the wheel of life, there are consequences: addictions, obesity, illness and destitution. It's imperative that we question mainstream thinking.

For example, we allow ourselves to be brainwashed by marketing when we eat everything that is pushed on us. French fries, pizza, candy, soft drinks, large portions, obesity rates climbing at alarming rates and we don't stop to think for ourselves: "Do I want to look the way I will look if I eat this? "

How about asking yourself: "Do I want to pay the doctors bills I will pay to be this unhealthy?" What about your family?

If we are going to regain our physical dignity, we need to wake our minds and rouse our souls.

The fact that there are people out there who make fortunes filling us with fat, sugar and nicotine is the topic for another book, but right now it is up to us to say No. If we say No to the Takers and Greedheads, their game is over. On the other hand, if we roll over and say nothing, they win.

"No," says the warrior. "You do not have my best interests at heart. No, you are not going to take advantage of me."

Are you able to say No like a warrior? If not, why not? Are you fearful? Of what? The number one answer I hear to this question is fear of confrontation.

We're adults now. We are in a position to rewrite the rules and to clear out the ghosts of confrontation. Confrontation doesn't have to include yelling, fear, physical threats, disapproval or anything else we may associate with it that makes us fearful.

Many of us who were raised with raging, or disapproving parents have vowed never to be like our parents. Problem is, we stuff our anger.

And more times than not, if we're stuffing our anger, it may come out in the form of passive-aggressive confrontation. In other words, we stab people in the back in order to avoid speaking our truth to them.

Usually, no one-- including us-- knows what's happened, because our anger "comes out sideways." It doesn't address the real issue, and, as a result, the real issue is never resolved and continues to rear its ugly head.

We have to be able to confront the takers in our lives. Otherwise, they sabotage our lives. If we can't confront the takers, we can't care for the people who want to love us.

Stop the Drama

Client: I've got a new woman in my life. She's exciting, passionate, athletic, and successful-- all the things I've always said I want in a partner. My ex must sense that I am moving on, because she keeps calling with different "stories" about why we should get together.

It's funny how, before I met this woman, my ex never called, but now she calls all the time. She stops by my office, and suddenly she 'just wants to be friends." I don't want to hurt her, and maybe she does just want to be friends, but the timing is suspect.

Therapist: The good news is your read is probably dead on. When exes suddenly appear around the time that you are moving on, it's no accident.

Consciously or unconsciously, many people don't want us to move on. They have their own insecurities, which become aggravated when others around them "move on."

It is up to us, and us alone, to say No to the people who want to sabotage our success.

I recommend a call, something of this nature:

Hi Ex! How are you? I wanted to let you know that I am in a new relationship, and I'm very excited about getting to know this person.

Right now just isn't the right time for me to be working on a friendship with you. I appreciate the gesture, and maybe sometime in the future, when we are both happy and solid in new relationships, we can see if the four of us might want to have dinner together. Thanks for understanding and respecting my wishes.

It is always amazing, even to me, how many people do not want to put healthy closures on past relationships. Sometimes I guess we want to keep someone "in the wings," just in case the new relationship doesn't work out. But there is a difference between an ex who is now a friend and an ex who is now a hanger-on.

Say no to safety nets and hangers-on.

Drama and Abuse

More times than not, I believe people hang on to past relationships, particularly bad ones, because relationships that are dysfunctional involve more drama.

Unfortunately, when someone has spent a lot of time in dysfunctional relationships, they become addicted to the drama. They actually start to think a healthy relationship or a healthy partner is boring... ho hum!

But that's backwards. Our relationships shouldn't be full of drama. Life comes with enough excitement and challenges. Instead, our relationships should support us and protect us through the drama that makes up the rest of our lives.

I have witnessed caring people take daring action to rescue someone from an abusive situation, only to find that the rescued person became angry with the people who "helped" him or her. Lawyers see it all the time when the abused refuses to testify.[v]

It is important for people coming out of an abusive situation to get help immediately. I recommend ongoing individual therapy, group therapy for abuse victims, and/or going away for several days to an intensive workshop dedicated to understanding what happens when we live with abuse and how to move forward from the abuse. Otherwise, we give in to feelings of grief, such as "I think about it. I miss it. I should be back there". No, these are the same feelings that accompany any loss. These feelings are not a sign that you should return to the situation.

Once we get over this, however, and discover what life has in store for us outside the domain of abuse, the difference between an exciting life and a life filled with drama becomes crystal clear.

Homework

When we live with abuse, it becomes our focal point: how much, when it will happen, how we can avoid it, maybe we're bad, maybe we're not, maybe we cause it, maybe we don't.

Is it exciting? Interesting? Ask yourself this, and answer yourself honestly: Is it interesting to your friends to hear about it?

Ending Drama and Abuse

Step One is getting out. If the abuser can get her spouse out of therapy, odds are better she can keep him trapped.

Step Two is staying out. While it will feel like a gigantic magnet pulling you back, you have to resist. You might miss the intensity most of all. "This is so boring," you'll tell yourself. "It may be healthy, but it sure is boring."

Step Three is to reinvent you-- quickly. Find a new job or, if you like your current one, immerse yourself in it. Travel. Take on a hobby. Whatever it is, find a passion, because, if she can find you, she will.

And when she does, you will want to go with her, because it feels good to be pursued. But as soon as you regain your self esteem, get a renewed interest in a healthy life, are not attracted to drama and time passes, you will find your ex's advances irritating. She will become a nuisance. Just the idea of more of her dramatic bullshit will be enough to set you off.

Leave me alone, you will scream, and you will wonder how you ever put up with the abuse.

Set standards for yourself. As soon as you do, it will no longer feel good to be pursued. It will feel more like "Fatal Attraction," someone is trying to intimidate you, threaten you, interfere and subvert you.

"No, I do not want to be with you. Thank you for asking."

Remember, the abuser can be male or female. Both are equally clever in how they keep you in their web. And remember, there are organizations, the sole purpose of which is to protect you and help you out of an abusive relationship.

Two Worlds

Of course, while it is illegal in this country to physically abuse one's children or wife, many people still live under the notion that wives and children are the property of the head of the household. They also believe they can treat their "property" as they did in their country of origin.[vi]

Often, all it takes is for two worlds to meet—the world of abuse and the world of talking—for the tide to begin to turn, as it did for this 16-year old boy who landed himself in the hospital.

Client: I know the nurses called you to come talk to me, because they heard my dad yelling that he was going to beat me when I got home. I know you are a nice lady who only wants to help, but let me tell you, I am from a very close family that takes care of itself. We don't want help from 'the system.' My dad's dad hit him, my dad hits me, and that's just the way it is. You're not going to change him. He doesn't even speak English very well.

Therapist: Unfortunately, in this country, if your Dad hits you, there are consequences. Maybe we can all meet and talk things out, so he doesn't have to resort to hitting. You must be the translator. Make sure he understands everything I say, please.

Client: Ok, but I am not optimistic.

Therapist: I am!

Meeting in the hospital with family, therapist and nurses waiting anxiously outside the room.

Dad was a fisherman…. an extremely honorable profession in his town and culture and a profession where sons followed their fathers making it a family profession. Dad had a new fishing boat and was taking it out for the first time. His son, left at home, not wanting to go to school, wanting to work by Dad's side on the new fishing boat had a party because he knew Mom would call Dad to come in to get things under control. The boy was, in fact, acting out, because he wanted to be out on the boat with Dad. At the party he accidentally physically injured himself and ended up in the hospital. In the session, after Dad yelled at his son for the party, his son was able to tearfully tell his Dad what he really wanted. Dad in tears tried to explain that he wanted his son to finish school before he started fishing, but secretly was honored his son wanted to be with him.

The meeting was the first to show this family that talking is more powerful than hitting. It was very emotional for all of us.

Client: I saw you crying. My Dad likes you for a 'system lady.'

Therapist: Thanks. Tears and talking are good.

How did we get here?

You may ask yourself, well, how did I get here?

-Talking Heads[vii]

What happens in our lives that we develop this inability to say No? To avoid confrontation at all costs? It's not as if we're born with it. Babies, for example, have no problem sealing their lips, turning their heads, and pushing spoonfuls of food away.

When we're raised in an environment in which parenting is compromised or essentially nonexistent, it is common for the child to become the parent.

We become competent in areas we wouldn't and shouldn't be. We stand on chairs to reach the cupboards for food for our siblings and ourselves. We stay at home to watch over our drunken dad and clean the house, instead of playing with the other 8-year-olds.

We lie about why we want to stay home, why we don't want our friends (if we still have any left) to come over, and why we always walk or bike to school, instead of being dropped off like all the other kids.

We pretend we're not hurt when Dad Indian burns us to exert abusive power, and pretend we're not scared when Mom drives us drunk. We pretend we can drive at an early age because we think we are a better driver sober at age 10 than Mom is drunk at age 40.

These become our standards. We don't say No because we can't say No. If we do, we think we will perish, one way or another.

Instead, we become overachievers: cleaning the house, feeding the children, enduring pain, driving. We develop a tolerance for toxic behavior.

Often times, things are so intense, and there's so much to do that we don't even know that what is happening in our house is not the norm in other houses.

To what extent are we, as children, willing to go to help our family?

I consulted with a 16-year-old girl who was admitted to the hospital because she was cutting her wrists, but she wasn't suicidal.

What she wanted was to get into the "system," in the hope that the system would be able to help her Dad who was drinking himself to death. (Dad had an incurable disease that he was treating with alcohol. He would tell anyone that wanted him to stop drinking he wanted to die rather than stay alive with this disease.)

She told me that her Dad would come home drunk at 2 am with sub sandwiches for them. He would wake her so they could eat their sandwiches, talk, and be together. Mom apparently had declined the sub sandwich gathering.

Client: I am often tired at school because I have to get up at 2 am when my Dad comes home from the bars with sub sandwiches and I don't want him to eat alone.

Therapist: Do you know that other 16-year-olds are not eating sub sandwiches with their dads at 2 in the morning?

Client: I didn't, but I think you may be right.

Dad had the right idea in that he wanted to spend time with his daughter, because he was checking out, just inappropriate time and conversations (drunken). When I told him if he was going to keep drinking in order to die he had to get up every morning early and sober to be with his daughter. He had to answer all the questions she might have of him:

Who is going to walk me down the aisle when I get married?

What type of a man should I marry?

Should I go to college or right into my profession (she was a superb dancer)?

What should I do if my husband drinks too much?

How can I take care of Mom and pursue my dancing?

Dad actually stopped drinking for some time after being given this assignment to do sober.

If we were raised with abuse, addictions or dysfunction, it may not have been safe to say No.

Client #1: My husband is a good man. When he drinks too much, it is a little difficult for all of us in the house. Last week, he came home drunk and threw the two older girls' beds out of the window because their bedspreads were crooked. He is pretty strict, and when he is drunk it is worse.

Therapist: Does he hit your children?

Client #1: No, just me. He doesn't hit me if my little one is in the room. She rarely leaves my side. I don't think she knows why she stays by me, do you honey?

Client #2: No. I like to be with my Mommy.

Therapist: Protecting you is a big burden for a 6-year-old Mom. Are you drinking as well?

Client #1: Yes, it helps me deal with the situation.

Therapist: It may feel like it helps you deal with the situation. It actually makes it worse.

Client #1: I think you may be right. I am here in your office for the first time because I think you may be right. I need to make my home safe for all of us.

Therapist: This may be your toughest and most rewarding journey. You do not have to live with this abuse. With sobriety and recovery, you and your family can regain your dignity, live in a safe home, and live your lives. If your husband wants to join you in a sober, dignified, recovering home, he will have to abide by the new standards. Beds will not be flying out of the window and six year olds will not be security officers.

The first step, of course, is to remove ourselves from a situation in which it is physically unsafe to say No. Once we're out of that sort of situation, it is time for us to begin to learn how to say No.

As we progress, there are four signs we can use to monitor our progress. They tell us when we're saying Yes when we should be saying No:

- Resentment
- Anger when others make requests of us. You want what?
- Out-of-character blowups.
- Avoiding relationships

Resentment

Resentment is "you owe me." If we make an agreement, money for a car, and I give you the car, but your check bounces, I am going to build resentment if I don't take action to have you fulfill your part of the agreement. This is the easy one. If however I "make up" that you owe me e.g. my parents should have been the model parents, or I paid last time so you should pay this time, or I am nice so you should be nice to me and on and on then I will also have resentment based on ideas I made up.

Resentment is a feeling with which we want to become intimate. It provides instant feedback, and therefore is a very valuable tool. Embrace it, and it will help you start taking care of yourself.

Sometimes, we think we're capable of saying No, when, in fact, we're not. Any time we find ourselves harboring feelings of resentment, there's a good chance we've been saying Yes when we should have been saying No.

Client: I am always paying for things. If I go to lunch with my friends, I always pay and they never reciprocate. Same with my husband. I see to all his needs. I do nice things for him every day. He never does anything nice for me. He doesn't even thank me. At this point, it's like he expects it-- just like the people I go to lunch with. People take me for granted.

Therapist: Are you asked to pay or do you offer? Does your husband ask you to do those things, or do you just do them?

Client: I just do them, because I think it's the nice thing to do. No one asks me. I keep thinking someone else will pick up the bill the next time, but they never do. I keep thinking my husband will think of me, but he doesn't.

Therapist: Do you think you are guilty of this crazy thing we women do? We give and give and give, build resentment and then we give some more.

Client: Ick. That sounds just like me.

Therapist: You're not alone. How about we try life a different way? There's nothing wrong with giving, so how about if you only give to the point at which you have absolutely no expectations that anyone will give back to you?

In other words, give only to the point at which you can do so without resentment. When you start to feel resentment, you have to stop giving.

For example, the next time the bill comes, define your terms, set your standards: I'll get this one, you get the next one. And when that time comes, it won't be such a surprise when you say; I think this is yours I got it last time.

If you're uncomfortable with that, it's okay. You could also say, Let's split it, then work your way up to a point where you're comfortable saying, I think this is yours. I got it last time.

You want what?!

If we feel anger when others make requests of us, it's another sign that we're probably having difficulty saying No. Like resentment, if we pay attention to anger, we can learn a lot about ourselves.

Client: I hate being around her. She is so pushy. Every time I'm with her, she gets me to volunteer for something I don't have time to do. I'm not going to the luncheon because SHE will be there.

Therapist: No one can get you to do things you don't want to do, except you. Have you ever said no to her?

Client: No, because I feel like I am a bad person if I don't help out, particularly a charity. What would people say? I don't care. Actually, that's not true. I care too much.

Therapist: Being able to say No to things you don't have time for has nothing to do with the charity. It's about knowing your schedule, your commitments, your priorities, and what you have time for.

Client: What do I say?

Therapist: Thanks for asking, Ms. Pushy. I can't help this time around. Please try me in the future.

Client: Are you kidding? If I can tell her No once, I'm not going to invite her to ask me again. You must be nuts.

Therapist: Probably. But it's good practice. Welcome other people's requests too, anybody's. Think of them as target practice. If you can respond with a No, it's the equivalent of a bulls-eye.

Blow-ups.

If we blow up from time to time, it's often because we feel like we haven't done anything for ourselves, only others. It's important not to dismiss our anger, but to give its source some thought. It might have a message for us: that we've been saying Yes when we should have been saying No.

We might end up in a fight with our wife about why she hasn't done the laundry. At first, we might think we're pissed about not having any clean shirts, whereas the truth is we are probably stressed from the money the business is losing, the unhappy customers we talk to regularly, and the long hours we are working.

Client: I'm running a short temper these days. Everyone seems to notice: my kids, co-workers, and my wife!

My kids even brought me my meditation shawl the other day—I had just gone off on them. I think it's because I'm stressed out and not taking care of myself. I'm not working out. I haven't meditated in months.

Therapist: Okay, let's make a schedule that is designed to have success. What is the minimum you will do, no matter what—workout, meditate? Let's start with manageable goals. That way, you're more likely to increase that minimum every week.[viii]

It is important for you to stop absorbing the stress of life. Push back. I can't talk to you today. How about tomorrow at 2 pm? I will be in late tomorrow. Here is what you have to do to open the business. No we can't spend money on that, we have to cut back for the next couple of months until the business is more solvent.

Homework

What arrangements can you make so that you can say No to someone else, in order that you can say Yes to yourself? All of us need to say yes to ourselves.

Where's Waldo?

People-pleasers often disappear rather than have an honest conversation, which may include saying no to someone.

Client: I was dating this great woman. I loved being with her, and I loved whom I was when I was with her. You know what I mean?

We were together 6 months. Then, because my friends thought I should be with someone else, I just didn't call her one day. Now it's been over a month. I miss her, and I don't know what to do. At first, I thought my friends were right, but now I don't know.

Therapist: Well, you have two issues: you need to think for yourself and you need to be able to have authentic conversations.

Client: I didn't want to hurt her and I didn't know what to do, so I did nothing.

Therapist: Doing nothing hurts more than having an authentic conversation.

Client: What do I do now?

Therapist: Friends can sometimes help us to see a toxic situation we might not have otherwise. Unfortunately, friends can also be self-serving and not want their friendship with you altered. They don't want to lose their wingman. You have to sort out what you think your friends are doing.

From the relationship you are describing, I think their recommendation might not have been in your best interest. So your first conversation is to tell your friends, thanks for sharing and I will take it from here.

After that, you call this woman and tell her the truth. Tell her what happened, what you have done about what happened, and invite her back into your life. If she is available, and feels you can make it safe for her, she might give it another shot. If not, you will have at least cleaned up the mess you made.

Many people have lots of messes that have never been cleaned up because they choose to do nothing vs. having an authentic conversation.

Homework

How were you raised? Were you taught what most girls were? To always be nice, always do what others want, and always say yes?

Or were you raised to speak up?

Raising the Stakes on Raising our Daughters

The new message for women is that relationships are partnerships: You do have a vote. Your opinion matters. Be a partner.

What message are we sending our daughters? Do they see us living day-to-day in a partnership? If not, how are they going to be anything but compliant when they start to interact with the opposite sex or chat on the Internet (with or without your permission)?

If a young woman has witnessed her mother allowing abuse, it may be hard for her to set her own boundaries. Sometimes these young women "coach" their Moms to be tougher with abusive Dad, but unknowingly allow abuse in other areas of their lives: teachers, coaches, their brothers' friends.

Sometimes women give up good jobs to move where their boyfriend wants to live, only to have the relationship go south: The boyfriend has a new girlfriend, and she has no job. Be smart and take care of your finances.

Women aren't necessarily taught to have difficult financial conversations. "Men handle that." Well, in the world today, women work and women need to get comfortable having conversations about money.

If you are complaining about a financial arrangement you have made with someone, it's up to you to know the number it would take to have you not complain. Do not say, "What do you think I should want?" which is a classic people-pleasing comment.

Just thinking about having financial conversations may make you feel sick. Well, think about how sick you are going to feel with an empty wallet. Learning to have financial conversations just takes practice. The first one is awkward, and the 2,000th one is like slicing warm butter.

I believe, when we lie to ourselves, it will eventually show up in our bodies. Put another way, our emotional selves will always be reflected in our physical selves.

The Posture of People-Pleasing

I know a woman who was in an abusive relationship for seven years. When she finally got out, a large tumor was discovered in her throat. Thank goodness it wasn't malignant, but she was lucky. She swears the tumor manifested itself in her throat because that's where her stress was: she couldn't speak her emotional truth.

Our emotions are present in our posture, which is different when we're speaking authentically than when we're not, for example, when we're saying Yes when we mean No.

When we are in the posture of any form of people-pleasing, our body follows our mind in searching for the right thing to say. If we separate ourselves from our emotional truth, we're not grounded. How can we be?

"What does this person need from me?"

"How can I get this person to like me?"

"How can I take care of this person?"

"How can I avoid conflict?"

Another set of conversations the people-pleaser is usually having:

"How can I fit in here?"

"I don't want anyone to see me."

"I am not worthy of having a different opinion."

"I don't want to rock the boat. I have to be nice."

Many people pleasers have explained to me that they get caught up in a vicious cycle of putting themselves down, which is why they need to please others. They are afraid if they speak up that the other person will come back with attacks on their behavior:

"Well, you didn't clean the house."

"You need to get your affairs in order."

"You don't exercise. You're overweight."

"Your family is crazy."

"You didn't finish school."

"You don't even have a job."

Whatever the people-pleaser's insecurities are, they are afraid those insecurities will be used against them if they stand up for themselves. They tell themselves they do not have the right to an opinion or to say no until they fix their own problems.

Do we have to be perfect, in order to have an opinion and to say No?

Of course not.

We use the same reasoning to put off change. It's not necessary that all of our affairs be in order before we begin taking care of ourselves, before we begin learning, for example, how to say No.

One client used her inability to afford our session fees as the reason why she couldn't immediately begin the process of learning to say No.

In contrast, a different client told me fees were no problem, as she now had money she hadn't counted on before. As a result of our sessions, she was developing the ability to say No in situations that previously had been costing her financially.

Do we ease into it, or go cold turkey?

It's your choice, really.

I worked with one client who found it easier to ease into saying No. In this case, it was a man, and he took the first step of saying, "I don't know" to requests.

Then, when he would arrive home, away from the person he felt he had to people-please, he was able to ask himself, "Do you want to do this?"

The answer was usually No. He was then able to go back and say No. This little tip of "I don't know" opened up a whole new world of being able to take care of himself.

For others of us, it's easier to counter. For example, "I'll bring you a cup of tea in five minutes." It's important not to over-emotionalize everything. A Yes or No is just that, an answer. Yes, I can. No, I can't. Or No, but I can do this.

Trust your intuition and don't idolize professionals! Remember the TV ad? I know a man who had a medical condition for two years. During that time, two physicians recommended major surgery, which he declined.

Finally, he visited the teacher of both doctors, only to be told, "No way, you don't need surgery. Take this pill." He did, and the condition cleared up in three days. Trust your authentic, intuitive self.

Trust your physical self, too.

Homework

If you assume a strong physical posture, it can help provide the backbone, both literally and figuratively, that you will need to speak authentically.

You want your feet to be firmly planted on the ground with your legs strong and your core at its optimal strength in order to emanate courage and confidence. Hold your shoulders back, keep your head high, and have your voice ring clear and strong.

"No, thank you for asking."

You can practice in front of the mirror. First, have the conversation: "Yes sir, no sir, how high sir," and watch your posture. Notice the physical posture of you abandoning you!

Then assume a posture of strength and have the conversation, "No, thank you for asking. These days, I am honoring myself and my concerns."

You might find it more your style to work with a friend. Working in front of a mirror, go back and forth for at least 30 minutes. First, have your friend make requests of you to which you respond with Yes's and No's, taking notice of your body's posture when you say Yes, then No. Make sure you are not offering stories, reasons or excuses when you say No.

Then make requests of your friend, to which he or she also responds both ways. Start with easy scenarios and move to real life situations. Work toward scenarios of sex and money. These are where many people have the hardest time.

Eventually, you may want to journal your reactions. What was the physical posture, and what emotions accompanied it? I have had people report wobbly knees, upset stomach, unresponsive voice, crying, etc.

Breathing, music, exercise and meditation are all ways to move through the physical reactions.[ix] It is always important to sort out our physical reactions from our chatter. The chatter is just that: chatter. "You are not good enough. That's being selfish. You are a bad person if you say No. What would your mother say? Don't rock the boat. Don't upset anyone."

We can thank the voices for sharing, but in the end we need to decline to listen to them. Our physical reactions can be lessened or alleviated with exercises or movements. For example, deep breathing can quiet everything down. Music and dancing can get us out of low-key anxiety. Exercise can tire us out. And long time meditators know they can quiet the body and the mind with serious practice.

You might want to take it in stages. It's almost always easier to reach a goal when it's broken down into smaller goals.

> **Goal One:** I will be more aware of how, when and where I take care of others at my own expense, where I say yes when I mean No.

> **Goal Two:** I will identify my concerns, beliefs, wants and needs, and say No to things that don't support me.

> **Goal Three:** I will develop standards for how I will allow myself to be treated. I will say No to anything that doesn't meet those standards.

Goal Four: Each week, I will find an opportunity to stop taking care of someone else at my own expense. Each week I will say No at least 1-20 or more times.

Goal Five: I will always, every minute of every day, take a stand for my beliefs, my concerns, and me. I will only represent myself, not everyone else in the world. I will learn to say No as easily as I say yes.

Developing our authentic self is like learning a forehand in tennis. Our first forehand is different than our 2,000th forehand, and all the forehands between 1 and 2,000 have a life of their own.

Some we'll hit too hard, and the ball will fly out of the court. Others we will mishit, and some we will miss entirely.

Sometimes when people begin saying No, they are more forceful, maybe because they are not sure it will work. Others might be too quiet: "What did you say?" "I said No!" Just keep practicing. The goal is to develop an inner knowing, an awareness, of what is going on with all of our interactions.

Ultimately, we develop the ability to know when and what to speak. We find the courage to actually speak authentically. We may even develop the ability to have real silence based on our truth not on our inability to speak.

All this may seem like a very involved process. Who wants to engage in all that thinking, expend that sort of energy just to have a conversation? The fact is, we already are.

Remember the people-pleasing process?

We suppress our own ideas, which we may or may not even know after so many years of suppressing them.

1. We attempt to read the mind of the person to whom we are talking.

2. We fabricate and articulate an idea that will lead to our being liked and avoid confrontation.

3. And, as if that isn't enough, this process leads to our expending further energy in the forms of:

    a. Judgmentalism
    b. Resentment
    c. Anxiety.

That's more than a full, five-set match worthy of energy expended, and it's all negative. We're going to expend energy as we learn to say No, but at least it's energy in a positive direction.

With time, the thought process will become unnecessary, and we will work by instinct, the same way experienced tennis players do.

We will have confidence in our ability to take care of ourselves in the domain of NO. "Thank you for asking, I cannot do as you have requested."

And then we will see all kinds of things begin to change.

We will attract a different kind of partner. Being empowered to be whom we truly are is very seductive to other emotionally strong people. Conversely, not having a sense of self, can be a magnet to those who need to control, abuse, or take advantage of others.

Sex and No

We will enjoy sex more. So many women I interviewed said they said yes to sex when they really just wanted the sex to be over and the person to go away.

Think about this phenomenon for a minute. Your body is very special. It is your body. No one should be allowed to touch your body without your permission, and deep down we all know this.

Conversely, imagine what it's like to want someone to touch your body. What a tremendous pleasure.

Client: I have definitely used sex to get people to like me. I have had sex because I was afraid to say No. How many times have I had sex just to get the person to go away? Countless. I even gained weight so that I wouldn't be attractive to people.

Therapist: Do you understand that no one has the right to touch your body without your permission? Do you understand that No means "No, thank you, I don't want you to touch me right now?" Do you understand that you are worth learning how to say No to unwanted advances? Do you understand not learning how to say No puts you at risk in the universe? Gaining weight, you don't want, to say No is you abandoning you! Stop! Learn how to say No!!!

As you learn what is important to you in the world, life slows down and is easier. You don't have to try all those beauty creams, because you know the one that really supports your skin.

You don't go through the buffet line, because you know what you want to order off the menu.

You don't have all those people around you, as they were only around because you were so accommodating. Instead, your entourage supports you for who you are and not for who they want you to be.

You have trusted friends who know you want to only hear the truth from them, because you welcome honest feedback. And they welcome the same from you.

Life gets easier and more enjoyable. As a matter of fact, the anxiety juice that used to come when you were afraid of rocking the boat or being a "pain in the ass" is replaced by warrior juice that makes you a more passionate, alive, and sought-after person.

Endnotes

---

[i] Allison Callaway, *Deaf Children in China* (Washington DC: Gallaudit University Press, 2000), 37.

[ii] Leonard Zusne and Warren H Jones, *Anomalistic Psychology: A Study of Magical Thinking* (New Jersey: Lawrence Erlbaum Associates, 1989), 13-15.

[iii] Seth Allcorn, *Codependency in the Workplace: A Guide for Employee Assistance and Human Resource Professionals* (New York: Quorum Books, 1992), 11.

[iv] *Pray the Devil Back To Hell,* Abigail E. Disney and Gini Reticker, Fork Films, 2008.

[v] Einat Peled, Zvi Eisikovits, Guy Enosh, and Aeev Winstok, " Choice and Empowerment for Battered Women Who Stay: Toward a Constructivist Model, " *Social Work* 45, No. 1 (2000): 9.

[vi] Renee Brant, "Case Vignette: Child Abuse or Acceptable Cultural Norms, " *Ethics @ Behavior* 5, No. 3 (1995): 283.

[vii] Talking Heads. *Once in a Lifetime on Remain in Light* (audio cd). Burbank, Ca: Distributed by Warner Brothers, 1980.

[viii] Kandra Strauss, "Dumping the Stress by Getting Fit," *National Education Association* 20, No. 7 (April 2002): 35.

[ix] John P. Miller, *The Contemplative Practitioner: Meditation in Education and the Professions* Connecticut: Bergin @ Garvey, 1994), 51-54.

Chapter Three

Making Requests

For the people-pleaser, the act of making a simple request can be as difficult as asking the hijackers of Flight 93 to please reconsider.

Countless clients with whom I've worked have somehow made it through the vast majority of their lives without making requests.

Some of us feel as if we shouldn't have to make requests, particularly of those with whom we're close. "If I have to ask," we tell ourselves, "it takes away from the experience." WRONG.

No one's a mind reader, and if we believe that people should know what we need, we will suffer endless disappointment and, ultimately, resentment.

That's why so many of us feel resentment toward our bosses. Typically, the issue is money-- specifically, we don't feel we're being paid what we deserve. But do we request more? No. Never.

Other times, wives are resentful of their husbands, and money is often the core issue. "Have you asked your husband for more?" "Oh no, I couldn't do that."

Patterns like this are deep-seated. The roots are planted during childhood.

For instance, I remember my first visit from a divorced mother seeking to improve her daughter's visits with her father. When I asked what would happen if the daughter made requests for activities she enjoyed, she responded:

Client: "If she ever made a request, he would hit her."

Hitting a child because she made a request would also train a child not to make a request. Now look closely with me here. Children are smart, and so-- without knowing what or why-- this particular girl, 7 years old at the time, had learned not to make requests.

Now fast forward as a young adult, she will feel tremendous resentment (she already at 7 years didn't like visiting Dad). She wouldn't know what she didn't know. She will have no idea that she is not making requests, and no idea that, by doing so, she could help end her suffering and unhappiness. Until she put herself in front of a wise therapist she might not know what was broken and how to fix it. This not knowing can be called a blind spot and will interfere with her emotional development from this point forward until this blind spot is revealed to her.[i]

Remember the little girl who shadowed her mother whenever her father was present, subconsciously protecting her mother?

She didn't know she protected her Mom from being hit by doing that but she knew something because she never left Mom alone in her Dad's presence when she was awake.

Children are wise adaptable little beings who take care of the family often at the expense of their emotional health. How does she protect people as a young adult? Again this will be a blind spot for her, needing to be revealed for her emotional health.

There are countless examples of children "keeping" their Mom in their bedroom so Mom doesn't have to go back to her bedroom with Dad. There are examples of children "unwilling" to leave the Master Bedroom because of some dysfunction they feel they are addressing by their presence.

How about the little girl who had to stand on the stool to reach the food in the cabinets in order to feed herself and her siblings? She has been trained to "take care of herself and others."

Or the girl whose parents purposely denied her requests? She learned people would hurt you if you give them the secret information about what is important to you.

Do you think these children grew up feeling comfortable making requests?

Or did they grow up with a tolerance for toxicity?

We are nothing if not creatures of adaptation. We work out, and our muscles adapt to the new stresses placed on them. We study, and our brains adapt to the new stimuli. These maladaptions all have the potential to become blind spots.

We adapt to our surroundings in a way best suited to our survival. If, as children, we adapted to take care of others at the expense of our emotional well-being, then that is exactly how we will take care of our family when we become adults ourselves.

Blended Families

Take blended families, for example, those in which the children of divorced parents are absorbed—or, more significantly, not absorbed--into a new family with new siblings and new stepparents.[ii]

How likely is it that these children are going to feel comfortable making requests? What challenges do they face? Even after they become adults, the challenges faced by children of blended families can be almost insurmountable.

We all know the story of Tim McGraw discovering that his real Dad was Tug McGraw, the legendary pitcher for the New York Mets and Philadelphia Phillies. [iii]

Tim's Mom had conceived him out of wedlock, and, as the story goes, when Tim finally met Tug, his Dad basically told Tim he wanted nothing to do with him.

By not responding to Tim's phone calls and letters, which amounted to requests for acknowledgment and a father-son relationship, Tug was, in essence, saying, "Let's pretend that night never happened." Well it probably comes as no surprise to you; I don't support this message.

Fact is if we are the parent of a child, we are the parent of a child. We may choose to have someone else raise that child e.g. adoption, and that is a responsible alternative to parenting yourself. But it's still our responsibility to see that process through.

Specifically, when we create a child with another person, it is our responsibility to acknowledge the child, see to it that the child is raised in a home in which it is safe to make requests, as well as to say No and to speak authentically.

It is not the child's responsibility that his parents created him. The child did not create himself. If we want to pretend otherwise, that is our burden to bear, not the child's. The child is innocent.

Instead, Tug's behavior sends the message that people need not take responsibility for their actions.

Client: My stepfather, since divorcing my Mom, has a new girlfriend, and we haven't seen him since she came on the scene. He hasn't called, hasn't acknowledged the boys' birthdays or any of the holidays. I'm hurt and I'm upset.

Therapist: Let's talk about what you see as your options and, conversely, what you have to lose?

Client: I want to send a strong letter requesting he get back to being the boys' grandfather, at the very least. I would also like to be part of his life with his new girlfriend, and that will take time.

He may say No, but I don't think I have anything to lose, since he's not in my life now anyway.

Therapist: Ok, let's go over the letter.

Clearly, this client had done her emotional homework. She knew that, if her stepfather declined, it was his issue, not hers.

Remember, we can only make the request. We cannot control its outcome.

But we must make the request. Otherwise, we just build up resentment, which is exactly what this client would have done had she not written the letter.

This story had a happy ending. The stepfather actually felt honored that his stepdaughter cared enough to make the request and that she was willing to risk his saying No.

Other stories don't always have such happy endings, and that's far more common.

Client: My dad has remarried and wants nothing to do with his first family. My mom and dad had three children, and he is pretending we don't exist. We think his new wife, who has three children of her own, is pressuring him to disown us and disinherit us, and he doesn't have the balls to stand up to her.

Therapist: Do you understand what a serious betrayal this is to your family by your father?

Client: Yes. I think it's why I have such a hard time with men, and why I pick the damaged men I do. None of them are there for me.

Therapist: Bingo!

The client, a very successful young woman, eventually paid her dad a visit. She requested he be her dad and include her in his life. He declined and told her to forget he was her Dad.

Therapist: What did you say to that?

Client: Something along the lines of the oral sex better be pretty hot to be replacing three kids.

Personally, I thought it was more about the father lacking balls, but……..

When a parent abdicates responsibility so egregiously, I can applaud such an edgy comment as the one this client made. It shows backbone, and helps her stand in a place of knowing that she is not responsible in any way for his abandonment and betrayal.

Given that the divorce rate keeps rising, unfortunately we can only assume that there will be more and more of this type of betrayal. I really encourage children in this situation to take a stand for the truth.

"You are my Dad, and I am your daughter/son, and anything you make up to the contrary is just that: something you made up. I will not enable this behavior on your part."

At any time in one's life, the damage done by having a parent forget his financial loyalty and commitments to his original family is challenging. Here are a few examples:

Client: My dad had an affair, ultimately married Her, and bailed on all the financial promises he made to his children: college, in particular, because his new wife has a different philosophy (children should be on their own at age 18). Not only did he promise us a college education, he spent years insisting that our job was to get into the best college we could, and that his job was to pay. We are ready to go to college and have kept our part of the bargain and Dad's financial support is no where to be found.

Client: My dad remarried late in life, and changed his will so that his new wife received everything. After that, her children got everything. He stopped the traditional Christmas-time checks and any and all financial support we used to count on him for. He was afraid of being alone, so he agreed to all her demands. When he finally did become ill and couldn't mentally care for himself, the new wife asked us, not her children for money to care for him! Fortunately, we had the presence of mind to say No. We counter offered to take care of him ourselves which she declined. When he died, his Will confirmed he had more than enough money to provide for his health care. She just wanted more money for herself.

Client: My mom remarried, and her new husband thought I looked too much like Mom's first husband, my dad. He felt threatened, and told my mom to abandon me. She did!

Homework

The scenarios go on and on, but if you feel like you're getting the short end of the stick, as painful as it is it's worth it to make the request of your parent/s that they take responsibility for creating you and keeping their agreements.

A good conversation would be any conversation that addresses the new situation. Many blended families do not address how things are going to be different going forward and what is everyone's input. The conversation might include what the "new situation" looks like for both parties. What agreements have we had that we might have forgotten? What do we need to speak about going forward?

It doesn't matter what the response is, since you will be maintaining or creating your dignity with the knowledge that you took a stand for yourself. And you must remember, if any parent refuses to take responsibility for creating you, it is about his deficiencies not yours.

Parental Alienation Syndrome

As if all this were not enough, there is another damaging phenomenon called parental alienation syndrome that is also a by-product of divorce.[iv]

What happens is that one parent, subtly or not-so-subtly, turns a child against the other parent through lies and brainwashing.

If you feel this may have happened, or be happening to you, do your research. If you have unreasonable, judgmental anger towards one parent, ask yourself why.

Generally, around the age of 18, children begin to feel powerful enough (or at least less vulnerable) to start scouting around for the truth about their parents and the divorce. Do not believe one angry (covert or overt) parent's stories about another parent. Find out for yourself.

Ask questions. I know one man whose ex-wife spent her whole life turning the children against their father. The father spent years and lots of money fighting her in court, and the kids wouldn't speak to him.

Finally, he'd had enough, and let it go. When each child turned 18, he turned over all the court records to them so they could do their own research. He now has a relationship with his children, and they won't speak to their mother. Don't enable this egregious behavior as a child.

Do your own research. Parents should not use their children for their own insecure, self-serving purposes.

The ability to make requests is critical to ending people-pleasing, living authentically and walking with dignity.

We must not only be able to make requests of our family members, we must be able to make requests in every facet of our lives.

Where and When

Client: I'm on call to my boss 24/7. He calls me anytime, day or night. He is ADD-like and if he thinks about it, and it is important he thinks it is important to everyone else.

I know other people in the office who are making more money than I am, and they work fewer hours. I think I need to leave. I just don't know where I would go. Plus there are perks to this job that I don't want to lose.

Therapist: What would it take financially and benefit-wise for you to no longer feel resentment knowing he is going to call you 24/7?

Client: Well if I was making this amount and he did this for me, (I know he does this for someone else in the office), I could stay.

Therapist: Write that number down, whatever it is. Don't focus on any deals he might have with others who work for him. Ask him to pick a time when you can talk about work, and let him know your thoughts.

Put together several different scenarios, just in case he needs that kind of flexibility, but have the bottom line number in your head.

This client almost doubled her salary, and—far from feeling resentful—had a renewed motivation to be the best she could at her job.

When it comes to taking care of ourselves, we can't look to others and what they have or don't have. "She gets this, so I should have that." Instead, we must ask ourselves, "What is it that I need in order not to build resentment?" We also need to keep our emotions out of the conversation," you like her better than me." Just make your request!

Client: I make more money than my husband, and I am constantly paying for things I don't tell him about. He'd be upset if he knew the actual cost. Even though he has no idea, I can still feel myself building up resentment, and I know I'm the culprit.

Therapist: Do your homework. Figure out the expenses, budget, and decide what contribution you need from your husband.

Remember, if you are requesting something of a man in your life; be smart. Men like to solve problems. Don't get caught up with emotions, just make a clean request, like, 'I need ½ of your paycheck every month, or I need all of your paycheck every month,' and then set it up so that you don't have to ask every month, some sort of direct deposit, for example.

Client: I think he will be angry, because that number is a lot different from what I've accepted from him in the past.

Therapist: It is easy to see in retrospect the messes we have made by not making a certain request sooner or by backing down from a request we did make. And when we are working in the domain of money, there are going to be strong triggers for both people.

Remember these important distinctions:

It is always more difficult to ask for change when it's a break in routine. If there has been a breakdown, and we allow that breakdown to continue, we send the message that it is not a breakdown at all.

Then we have to own up, and admit that we made a mistake. I let you think it was fine, when, in fact, I have realized lately that it is not fine. I take responsibility for the past, but we need to start anew.

Identify the nature and difficulty of the conversation, and ask your partner to pick a time to discuss. Present all information, take responsibility for your part in the breakdown, and ask for what you need in order to not have resentment.

Allow the other person to have his say. Don't give up the conversation until you have resolution. It is okay to take breaks, but, if you don't want to lose that person from your life, keep revisiting the issue until you have resolution.

Financial Dignity

In some cases, though, resolution means that we've decided we're better off without a certain person in our lives.

Years ago, I was using an old school financial advisor. I would ask him why he chose a particular investment, what its particular advantage was over another one, why not this one, what about that one. In other words, I insisted that he share with me the thinking behind his advice, not just his advice.

Finally, he said to me, "You're supposed to just do what I tell you," and that was the end of our relationship.

I also ended a relationship with a Harvard doctor, whom I actually liked in some domains. But when I would attempt a dialogue with him about a solution to a particular physical breakdown I was experiencing, he refused.

"I don't know why you come to me," he said. "You don't just do what I tell you to do."

You know who else told his clients to just do what he told them? Bernie Madoff.

Requests made in the financial domain are tough, but we need to be able to make them. Sometimes they are as difficult as we would expect them to be, and other times they are surprisingly simple.

Client: I have three new clients in three different states! I get to work on new material, and I get to travel.

Therapist: Have you had the money conversation? Do they know your fee?

Client: No, I'm sure it will work out. These are all good people.

Therapist: No, actually it may not work out, if you and they have a completely different idea of what your fee is.

Client: Asking for money is so hard for me. What if they change their minds and don't want to work with me?

Therapist: Why would you give your services away when you have all these unpaid bills?

Client: I don't feel worthy. I am afraid they won't want to pay me.

Therapist: You are fabulous at what you do. Everyone is always telling you what a difference you have made in his or her life.

Remember this: People respect other people who respect themselves. This one idea is crucial to your success in life. You have actually managed to get through most of your life without making clean requests, and you have a history of feeling used and abused by people.

In spite of the fact that sometimes her requests went smoothly, this client continually struggled with asking for her fee. Sometimes, it would happen so easily she was stunned, but nevertheless, she dreaded and fretted that some requests might not be honored.

She always knew I was going to ask how her requests were going, and she knew it felt better when financial agreements were in place, but it continued to be a huge source of stress for her.

I recommended she hire someone to make the requests for her. We can't just pretend it doesn't matter. We either have to learn to ask for our money, or hire someone to do it for us.

You can't always hire someone, however. Take the most challenging request of all time, the Everest of requests, so to speak. What is it? Any request made in the sexual domain. Good luck hiring someone to do that for you!

Sex

So many men equate requests in this area as a reflection of their inadequacy. Women know this, don't want to offend, and so say nothing.

What is the end result? The man eventually finds out or figures it out, but it's thirty, forty or fifty years too late. Game. Set. Match-- it's over, but no one's won. He lost and she lost, all because no one would bring it up.[v]

For new couples, I recommend giving thought to questions like these:

1. Are you a match sexually?
2. Do you have similar sexual appetites?
3. Can you both talk about sex?

4.   In this domain I recommend focusing on the positive more than what is not working.

If neither partner wants to discuss sex, there is no need to worry about a breakdown. If one partner wants to discuss sex and the other doesn't, "Houston, we have a problem".

The longer a couple has been together, and the longer any sexual patterns have manifested themselves, the more difficult it becomes for one to address or change those patterns.

Problems usually present themselves when one person deviates from the pattern or becomes dissatisfied with the status quo and isn't comfortable addressing it in conversation.

Pregnancy and the birth of a child can often change a sexual pattern. Sometimes it is the man who might be nervous about having sex with his wife during pregnancy or after the birth of the child and sometimes it is the wife who is "so exhausted" she has no interest in continuing their physical life. Do not pretend you don't have a breakdown! Pick a time agreeable to both of you and start talking about a resolution.

Problems always present themselves when one partner feels the other should know what he or she wants and feels that making such a request would spoil it.

Remember, none of us are mind-readers. We need to let our partners know what we want. Requests provide the people in our life with roadmaps as to how we will be treated. Requests provide our sexual partners with a roadmap of how we would like our bodies to be treated.

We all grow and change, in all areas of life, not just sexually. It is not a sin to change, but it does present some challenges if we are uncomfortable making requests.

Family Celebrations

Client: He practically did nothing for my birthday. He put a card by my morning cup of coffee. We always had such big birthday celebrations when I was growing up. We pretty much celebrated our birthdays for a week with different presents every day.

Therapist: What is his history of birthday celebrations? If he doesn't know yours, he will probably do what he's used to.

Client: I don't know.

Therapist: Sounds like a good conversation to have-- the birthday conversation. Begin with an assessment of your histories: I liked this part, and I really didn't like that part. Then design how you want to celebrate your birthdays as a couple, and how you want to celebrate your children's birthdays.

This is a breakdown that can be handled with requests and negotiation. No one is wrong because they celebrated birthdays a certain way. There is no bad guy here. There is simply, 'Let's talk and figure out what we as a couple want to do.' This conversation can be had for all family celebrations.

Homework

Reflect on your history. If you grew up in a dysfunctional, addictive, abusive, or controlling family, for example, it may not have been safe to make requests.

If your childhood was about taking care of others, there may not have been room for requests.

Look at your life now. Do you live in an environment in which requests are tolerated?

Are you able to make requests of your friends and sexual partners, coworkers and employees, financial advisors and mechanics?

Often, people-pleasers hate to make requests because they don't feel worthy. They are afraid of rejection. A typical people-pleaser request sounds something like this:

"There's a great movie playing tonight."

That's it. That's the request. Translation: "Mary, there's a great movie playing tonight. Would YOU like to go with ME?"

Mary: "No, I can't. Thanks for asking. Maybe another time."

How great would it be if conversation were always that simple? It would be, if we were all Sioux warriors.

"Stands With Fist, would you like to go to the movies with me tonight? There's a new slasher film I'm dying to see."

Stands with Fist: "No, I can't. Thanks for asking. Maybe another time."

Request Role Models

In order to become a warrior, we need role models like Stands with Fist. I got lucky. My role model happens to be an old dear friend of mine. For him, making a request is truly as easy as a hot knife slicing through butter.

In spite of multiple surgeries, my friend became blind when he was just 17. I first met him when we were in our 40's.

He was working two businesses, one on the East coast, where he lived, and one on the West coast, so he traveled cross-country frequently. He had a wife, children, and a political appointment. He was a walking request.

When we went out to lunch, for example, he requested a synopsis of the menu. When the meal arrived, he requested specific placement of the food, for example: meat at 2 o'clock, please.

I loved being around him. He was authentic. He spoke his mind, and expected the same of those around him. It was easy to forget he was blind because of his ability to make requests to take care of this concern.

Requests Never Made

On the other hand, I worked with a woman who for two years had been sexually involved with a man who had never once asked her out on a date. They would both go drinking with respective friends, go home together at the end of the evening, and that's what they called dating.

But I didn't.

This client actually thought she wanted to spend her life with this man. I didn't think she even knew who this person was as a friend, let alone a life partner.

They had never really engaged in the game of life and love. He had never asked her to go to dinner; she had never asked him to pick her up, and so on. Given what life throws at families these days, I was not sure this couple would be suitably prepared.

Make Those Requests!

Mutual request-making is one of the signs of a healthy marriage. It is our way of giving our significant other a roadmap of how to take care of us, because we are all different. We can't assume that what makes us happy necessarily makes our partner happy.

When we find ourselves complaining about how we are treated in the world, we have to look at our part in the dynamic. We not only have to require of ourselves that we make requests; we have to look at whether our requests are being honored. Our requests let others know our standards. If we are honoring our standards we should have few complaints about how we are treated in the world.

Fear of rejection often keeps us from making requests. One client in particular told me that she would withdraw a request the second the other person hesitated.

We have to remember that when someone responds with a "No," it's no different than when we say "No" to them: It's not a rejection; it's an answer to a question. It is a statement about what you can or cannot do.

Homework

Make a list of where you think you are competent making requests and where you have difficulty. What do you notice?

Is your difficulty limited to the opposite sex?

Or is it with people with whom you're already close?

Is it money-related?

Is it work-related?

Is it in the domain of sex?

Then consider why it's difficult with those people or in those situations.

Here's a list of what other clients discovered about themselves:

1. I don't deserve to ask for anything.
2. People who do that are selfish.
3. Other people should be able to "mind read" and know what I want.
4. My religious training taught me to only think of others.
5. I need to be perfect before I can ask for me.
6. People will know what you want, and they can harm you.
7. People will know what you want, and they will not grant the request.
8. If I know it is important to me, I will be disappointed since my requests have never been honored.

Pick a person or situation with whom or in which you think it will be easiest to make some headway. Begin to make requests in a restaurant if that feels comfortable. Notice what you tell yourself about asking the people close to you to do something. One woman reported how uncomfortable she felt when her husband did something really nice for her. This is called difficulty receiving!

You're feeling better, aren't you, honey?

Many women never realize they have spoiled the people around them. When husbands and children become sick, Mom's always there with chicken soup, crackers, ginger ale and popsicles.

What a surprise it is to discover that when they, themselves, get sick, there's no one taking care of them.

If we haven't taught people to take care of us, we shouldn't be surprised when they don't.

Most families don't want to see Mother Earth on the couch, unable to serve them as she has for years. How many of us have had our husbands ask, "You're feeling better, aren't you, honey?"

What he really wants to know is, "You're feeling good enough to start taking care of us again, aren't you?" Do not be disappointed because you expected the same people you, yourself, spoiled, to take care of you when you, yourself, need taking care of.

I recommend Mom if you are going to have surgery, or you get sick, any situation where you need to count on others to take care of you; make requests of a community that you know can serve you. Ask a good friend, ask someone you pay-its her job to make and bring you chicken noodle soup, but ask someone you know will take care in the way you might. Observe if you have difficulty receiving.

Our children don't need to see us as martyrs; they need to be taught many of the chores that make a family run. If you wear a cape with an S that stands for Supermom, it is time to engage the rest of the family. Here's how you might start:

"It is time for us to understand better how a family works. There are certain things that have to happen every day, and I think it is time for all of you to pick the things that you want to make happen every day. I have made out a list, and I want you to pick off that list what you will do."

One client who tried this had two children, and she needed the groceries bought and the laundry done weekly. Each child picked what he would do.

She also told them they would have to do it together. They lived in a high rise in the city, where it was wise to be in groups rather than alone, so she felt safer if they were making a lot of noise together.

It also taught them to coordinate action with people. If one child wanted to be difficult and not get the groceries when the other child wanted to, he ran the risk of similar behavior when he wanted to do the laundry.

They did all the "fun" things kids do, such as push every button on the elevator when they got off (at the 20th floor!), bought groceries they wanted that weren't on the list, but they got everything done together.

With that one request alone, Mom, literally, was able to take those things off her plate, and the kids actually "enjoyed" the time they had together. Truth be told, they actually felt proud to be part of running the ship.

As these children matured and ventured out into the world, they met other people their age who had no idea how to take care of themselves in the domestic domain. The kids took further pride in teaching their skills to others.

Homework

Start making requests by vowing to make one request per day, one per week, one per month, whatever you want. But whatever time frame you choose, stick to it.

Learning to make requests is not like learning to say No. There's no easing into it. Our only option is to go cold turkey.

For example, when we say, "Please don't," how does one ease into that? Our request is either honored or it's not. We either want a raise or we don't.

The only opportunity we have to ease into this learning process is the time frame to which we vow to adhere, so pick one that's reasonable for you and the type of relationships you are in.

Each time you make a request, see what sort of obstacles or reactions are present, and keep a journal of these observations:

1. Any of the feelings expressed in the list above.
2. Physical reactions: voice stops working, knees shake, and tears.
3. Verbal reactions, for example, you withdraw the request.

Note any specific people in your world who do not allow you to make requests.

Note differences between making a request of one person versus another.

Remember to differentiate between chatter and physical reactions. Examples of chatter are: "You are not good enough. That's being selfish. You are a bad person if you ask for things. What would your mother say? Don't rock the boat. Don't upset anyone."

Examples of physical reactions are: stomach queasy, voice shaky or stops working, knees wobbly, tears etc.

Decline the chatter and physical reactions and make a request doing the salsa if necessary.

Take note of the feeling of strength and any other emotions when your first request is honored.

Success Story

Remember our young client who had been taken advantage of her whole life: she requested her new live-in boyfriend put together a contract with her where they both agreed to certain responsibilities: her suffering vanished. She felt empowered in a way she had never felt before.

Do you know when you begin to clear the darkness and suffering you have lived with so easily, you start to wonder why it took you so long. These are just conversations! These are effective powerful conversations but they are just conversations.

Remember the young woman who suddenly realized she didn't have standards for the way people treated her. You practically have to get a certificate that you passed standards to interact with her now.

Don't wait too long. When we start to regain our emotional health, we start to attract people who respect healthy people.

We begin to live a life where requests just flow, and before we know it, there will come a time where we just delivered ten requests and they were all granted or we survived the ones that were declined. Requests will become transparent.

Endnotes

i Colin Feltham and Windy Dryden, *Brief Counseling: A Practical, Integrative Approach* (England: Open University Press, 2006), 145-146.

ii Kimberly Davis, "Making Blended Families Work," *Ebony* 55, No. 12 (October 2000): 40.

iii "McGraws Search for his Father," *The Week* (November 13, 2009): 10.

iv Judith S. Wallerstein and Joan B. Kelly, *Surviving the Breakup: How Children and Parents Cope with Divorce* (New York: Basic Books, 1996), 77.

v Karen Winkler, "Kinsey, Sex Research, and the Body of Knowledge: Let's Talk about Sex," *Women's Studies Quarterly* 33, No. ¾ (2005): 285.

Chapter Four

Keep Going

Our first example is a woman who had a history of failed relationships. She also had hurt people because she violated the rule you have heard me repeat over and over. She didn't give people the opportunity to fight for their relationship because she left it emotionally for another person. She used an affair to leave a relationship in which she had given away all her power.

After doing a lot of work she is now able to bring up her concerns in her relationship, she doesn't bring in a third person, she can apologize and take responsibility for her mistakes and she can still become paralyzed if someone throws her history at her. "You always hurt people, I knew you would hurt me, everyone told me you would hurt me".

When you don't feel good about yourself at your core you are vulnerable to others' attacks. By developing your authentic self you are building positive self-esteem and beginning to eradicate the core of negativity and self-doubt.

Take a serious look at where you stand in the world. Are your eyes wide open?

Do you acquiesce with what in your heart of hearts you know is wrong because you don't have a backbone?

What do you want to say about yourself as you move through life? Do you want to stand for truth or lies?

If you had the courage to say anything, what would it be?

Are you "still" afraid of conflict?

Do you still allow people to brainwash you for their self-serving agendas?

If you could relive certain times in your life, what would you have done differently?"

What would you have said differently?

Now that you have been working with declining what is not in your best interest and asking for what is, what do you see? What do you see about where you have been and where you are going? What do you notice is different about your body?

Remember Julie's mom, whose daughter asked, "Why can't you stand up to Alison's mom?" Well, now her daughter is saying, "Mom, you have courage. You are strong. You think something, you say it." How good must that feel?

When we are afraid, we cower. Our bodies' shrink and our minds collapse, as mine did when I was mugged.

When we face the world as warriors, we unfold and expand.

Remember our knuckle-bleeding people-pleaser who now has standards? She likes to remember what it used to be like every now and then to appreciate what it feels like now. Some of the gifts of her knuckle bleeding hard work are: the freedom from the incessant negative chatter, the absence of suffering, and not overcompensating. She has a new sense of self, she is seeing her children act in healthier ways, and she knows it is a direct result of her changes.

Our young woman, who said No to her boyfriend's need to see other people, reported a surge of energy, newfound dignity and a new belief in the offer she is in the world.

Did these clients experience fear before having the new conversations or sadness if it didn't work out? Of course and they can move through those feelings. When you keep taking actions that continually produce resentment you don't move through the resentment, you live in it.

Many people report amazement at how fast they can move through issues that they use to suffer with for years.

Once we become warriors, life becomes easier, much easier.

For example, we have more energy, because we have less anxiety.

I know one woman who has delightful dinner parties. At the end of the dinner, she thanks us all for coming, says she knows we would like to help clean up but she likes to do it herself, and hopes we will all get together again soon.

The evening is over! She has boundaries, expresses them effortlessly, and no one ever has to guess when is the right time to leave.

Life also becomes easier as a warrior, because we have more money. Why? Because we have said No to takers:

"I consider you a friend, so I'd like to give you the discounted family and friends rate (not free)."

Life becomes easier as a warrior because we have fewer problems with our children. They become better people too, because we've become great role models.

Life is easier as a warrior. The hard part, however, is taking the steps to become one, and the most difficult step is before you now.

Learning to Speak Authentically

Researchers have found people are more effective in their interpersonal interactions when they are more open and aware of their blindness's.[i]

Researchers have also found people feel more comfortable being open when they trust. Understanding cultures can help manage expectations and trust in relationships. We have the culture of our family of origin, the culture of our gender, our heritage, our geographical location etc. An Italian male from New York lives in a different discourse with different expectations and standards than an adult female from El Salvador. We cannot assume everyone thinks the way we do. Trust increases the more we know about and understand others and ourselves.[ii]

In order to achieve warriorhood, we need to learn to speak authentically. Speaking authentically requires trust, respect, understanding of the person with whom we are speaking and learning the steps to have a successful interaction.

Speaking authentically can be more difficult than declining and making requests. We will look at more challenging scenarios for this exercise. Some of these situations don't necessarily have a right answer just a right answer for you. We are also going to look at situations where the people you might be dealing with are more difficult people.

People who are mentally fragile present different challenges. Often they can dish out nastiness but crumble into hysterics or tears if you speak authentically to them. Some people we feel can out talk us. How often have I heard "she is smarter than I am" she gets louder and uses big words and I get confused etc. Controlling people can become enraged if they feel the order they believe they need in the universe is threatened. Bullies use bullying tactics e.g. insults, minimalizing your concerns, making fun of you, sarcasm as humor etc.

Let's look at some guidelines for you to remember as you begin the journey of being authentic by having authentic conversations.

Guidelines for Learning to Speak Authentically

1. Identify the conversation you would like to have before you start, and both of you pick a time that is mutually convenient.

    "I would like to have a conversation about finances with you. What is a good time for you?"

2. Take breaks if you get tired or overwhelmed, or just want a break.
    "This was a good start. Let's take a break and get back to this conversation tomorrow."

3. Avoid name-calling and personal attacks.
    "You idiot. You are so stupid."

4. Compliment whenever possible. Acknowledge the other person's strengths.

    " You are such a good father, husband, wife, friend."

    "You care about us, you are a good communicator."

5. Apologize when it is indicated.

    "I apologize I didn't bring this up earlier."

    "I apologize I attacked you. I shouldn't have."

6. Avoid absolutes like "always" and "never."

    "You never compliment me."

    "You never help with the kids."

    "You are always working."

7. Register complaints in a respectful way if you feel you must let the other person know what they are doing wrong.

    "I don't like it when you show up at our home without letting us know you are coming."

8. Just make your request/ask for the new behavior.

    "I ask that you call us before you come to our home and we can all decide what is a good time."

9. Acknowledge the success of the conversation, negotiate, and/or agree to disagree.

"I understand you want to come to our home whenever it is convenient for you and that is not going to work. We want you to come two afternoons a week from 3-5 and we will agree to two afternoons from 2-5."

There won't always be time to prepare each and every conversation you have. Life, as you know, just doesn't work like that. Remember the guidelines and if it is possible to get the new behavior you are looking for without spending time on the behavior you don't like I recommend skipping 7 and just going right into 8.

"Hi, I'd like to talk to you about something new our family is doing. From now on we are asking people to call before they come over so we can all decide what are good times for visits."

The more you practice speaking authentically, the more likely it is the words you have to choose in a pinch will embody the spirit of the language in the guidelines above and the examples below.

You can practice in the quiet of your home, with a partner, however you like. We will start with some conversations that tend to trip people up. They are a good place to start.

Make sure you give yourself permission to speak authentically in the situations you care about to an audience you assess can handle your authenticity. Give yourself permission to speak your truth particularly in a situation where you are going to alter your behavior and do the opposite to what you promised.

For example, when most of us have a bad meal at a restaurant, we vow never to return. Not only that, we vow to tell everyone we know.

But what do we do when the server, host or manager asks us how everything was? We say it was delicious and that we'll be back.

Speak up. The restaurant wants you to come back. Give its staff a chance to take better care of you.

Learning to speak authentically can be taken in steps, which is to say we can practice in situations that are less demanding and in which less is at stake. We can then work our way up to situations that are stressful and on which there may be much more at stake.

For example, you might choose to start practicing at a restaurant you have never visited before, as opposed to one you frequent.

Real Life Examples 101

Waiter: How is everything cooked?

You: All of the meals are perfect, except I ordered my steak rare and it is medium.

Waiter: Thank you. We will fix that immediately.

Doctor: I think I can fix the problem you are having with surgery. I am available to do the surgery later this week. We have to move fast because I am a very busy man.

You: Thank you for getting me in so quickly. What I would like to do, though, is slow the process down a bit, take my records, and get a second opinion.

Doctor: Humph! Well, I may be too busy to see you by the time that happens."

You: Thank you for understanding what a major decision this is for me. I want to do my due diligence before signing on for surgery. Where can I get my records?

Landscaper: We can put all these trees close to the house for shade.

You: What if they grow so big they start to damage the house.

Landscaper: Oh, that won't happen.

You: Please put that in our agreement. It might take years for the trees to grow that big, and this way both of us will have a record of it.

You (later): Hi, we have a problem because what I was concerned about is now a reality. The roots of the trees are damaging the house. I am glad we wrote the agreement to include this concern.

Plumber: Well that should take care of everything. You should have hot water with no problems.

You: And if for some unknown reason I am standing in a cold shower what is your warranty for your work and let's get that in writing?

Contractor: I will be in charge of making sure everything gets done correctly and on budget, and for that, you pay me 10% of the total cost.

You: What I would like to do is sit down every week with you, go over what happened that week, what didn't happen and why, and where we are with the budget.

Financial Advisor: You will give us your money, and we will handle it from there.

You: I am a person who has gone from never asking questions to asking a million; so let me know if your firm can accommodate an interested investor who will stay on top of his portfolio by speaking with my contact person. If you don't work that way, I will find someone who does. Thank you.

Business Services: Signing Contract but Changed Your Mind after New Information Obtained: Ok, I will have all the paperwork drawn up by Monday for you to sign. We have put a lot of time into this agreement. After you sign we can move forward and you will give us your deposit.

You: We have done further research and have found someone who fits our parameters better. We have decided to sign on with their agency. We appreciate all the time you took with us. Thank you.

Dead-Beat Boyfriend: What do you mean where are we going? We are just hanging out and having fun.

You: Call me if you move from hanging out. (Read Steve Harvey's book: *Act Like a Lady, Think Like a Man*).

Eye-Roving Boyfriend: Whew! She's Hot!

You: Call me when you get your eyes fixed!

Controlling Husband Wanting Fast Divorce: I'll have my lawyer draw up a settlement and you will just sign it.

You: Send me an offer and I will review it with my team and get back to you.

Ex-wife/ex-girlfriend: I need you here Saturday morning at 9 am to help me load up these heavy things and take them to the dump. I don't have anyone else and I really need help.

You: Actually, that is not going to work for me. Thanks for asking.

Ex-husband/ex-boyfriend: I need you to be my escort at my office party this year. We can go as friends, and no one has to know. I just don't want to go alone. We had plans to go before we broke up. Everyone is expecting you to go. Please.

You: Actually, that is not going to work for me. Thanks for asking.

Unconscious, Controlling Friend: I signed us up for the course I want to do this weekend. Pick me up on Friday at 5pm.

You: Thanks; I won't be able to make it.

Difficult Parent in Long Term Care: Do you know I am always alone here on Sunday? All the other residents are out for dinner with their children. I am the only one here who never gets calls. Did you forget you had a father? So you finally found your way here.

You: Hi Dad! Let's go for a walk.

Disapproving Parent: Are you really going to leave your secure corporate job to start your own business?

You: Yes, and I hope you are happy for me, because I am really happy!

Disapproving Child to Parent: What do you mean you are moving to the islands? Who is going to babysit for us?

You: I am so excited about moving to the islands. It will be such fun when you visit.

Abusive Partner: I will teach you to never look at another man/woman again. Smack!

You: 911 - I have an emergency at 99 West Drive. Please come immediately!

Lawyer's Office: You must stay away from this abusive partner and you must testify!

You: I will and I will!

Advanced Real Life Examples

I have had many examples of enabling families who unknowingly keep their children dependent on them through money. Some parents keep their children on the payroll and attach conditions to the money. Other parents forget that their children have grown up and do not live in their home anymore. As your children are growing up your job continues to change as a parent. You must be encouraging your children to find their voice even if is different from your voice.

If you as a parent want to contribute to your children financially, you must do so without strings attached. Giving your children money doesn't give you a ticket to make their decisions for them. You had your turn to raise your family and you now must allow your children to raise their children!

Now, it does not mean that parents of grown children can never have an opinion about their children's families. It does not mean that children must exclude their parents from important decisions they are making.

If everyone is healthy and subscribes to autonomy, these conversations will be easy. There are plenty of philosophies on how to raise our children today.

There are lots of difficult waters to negotiate as a parent. Decisions need to be made in the domains of health, education, discipline, sports, etc. so why not discuss these issues with someone you respect and who has already been down this road? Discuss yes and it is the grown child's final decision with his spouse.

 If you have overbearing, intrusive, controlling parents, you may need to set firm boundaries. "Thanks for sharing parents we will take it from here."

If children on the other hand EXPECT their parents to continue supporting them after they are married, parents may have to set boundaries. One parent told me he thought the greatest gift he could give to his children was to take care of himself so they wouldn't have to. Parents, give because you have extra and you want to, not because you are a martyr or you want to control.

Let me be clear on what I am saying. I believe close families with healthy boundaries, supporting autonomy, are what our families and our country need today. In no way am I against close families. I just advocate they be emotionally healthy families.

Parents

Client: The only relatives that live anywhere close to us are impossible. They show up whenever it is convenient for them, with no regard for what we are doing.

They stir the pot by getting involved with difficult conversations we are having with the children. They try to turn the children against us. My husband and I are at our wits end.

He thinks we have to take a really tough stand, and I don't know if I am up to it. I keep telling myself that they are family, and maybe we are being too mean.

Therapist: If you and your husband are beginning to fight about this issue, then it is time to get on the same side. You have to set boundaries with people who are unhealthy for your family.

This will be very tough for you, because you don't like to hurt people and you want everyone to like you. I encourage you to stand united as a couple and use words like 'we,' 'my husband and I,' and 'my wife and I.'

You will have to decide what to do if they ignore what you ask them to do and disrespect your boundaries. What will you do if you ask them to come on Tuesdays from 3-5pm, and they come on Monday or won't leave at 5 pm on Tuesday?

Client: My husband says we have to be prepared to close the door on them or usher them out the door. He says he will do it if it is too hard for me.

Therapist: He is really being a partner to you in this breakdown. You need to be able to support him when he does the tough stuff. You cannot go against him in front of your relatives. Don't even start the conversation until you are totally united-- no matter what antics they pull.

Client: I can already imagine them telling the rest of the family how horrible we are, and how they just wanted to get together as family.

Therapist: And...

Client: I know, I know. I still want everyone to like me.

How do we handle volatile situations that require us to make tough decisions?

Two great examples of phenomenal child rearing are:

1. Anne Sullivan in *The Miracle Worker*[iii] and
2. Ray Charles's mother in *Ray*.[iv]

Neither could afford to be people-pleasers. Anne Sullivan had to prepare Helen Keller for dealing with her deafness and blindness. Her commitment and integrity so poignantly illustrated in the famous dinner scene where Anne confronts Helen's equally determined temper tantrums. Ray's mom who had to prepare Ray for his blindness demonstrates her commitment and tough love with the powerful scene where she says, "I'll show you how to do something once, I'll help you if you mess up twice, but the third time you're on your own. Cause that's how it is in the world."

Their courage, caring and perseverance made a real difference. Compare their actions to those of Cartman's mom in South Park.

Divorces

Client: My best friend is getting divorced, and she and her husband have always been our best friends. She has asked me to never talk to her husband again, because he has been so mean to her. What do I do? We don't support what her husband, also our friend, has done to her either, and it's a real conflict for us.

On top of it all, our children all hang out, so we're going to be at ball games together. It's not just about us. We want to do what's in the best interest of the kids.

Therapist: These situations never have one right answer. I think the best you can do is to go through a healthy process of thinking through your decisions.

For instance, what is your friend trying to accomplish by asking you to never talk to her husband? Is there a way to accomplish this with a different action? Is your friend asking you to never speak to her ex about how she is doing? You can certainly honor that. It is not your job to carry information about either partner to the other partner.

She may need a safe or comfortable place to react to this trauma. Both of you can also certainly let her husband know what you think about his behavior, and that in no way do you condone how he has left his marriage: affair, financial abandonment, lies, abandoning his children.

Since the children are young adults, you can have your own conversation with them: I'm sorry you are going through this divorce. We don't support your Dad moving on so fast, and understand that might be hard for you. We just want you to know we are here for you if you need to talk or are just having a bad day.

These are difficult situations, particularly when the community is a small one. Ask questions to help sort out how you can be the most sensitive.

The most important concept here is if you only people-please you will just do what you are told without thinking. A better solution: You and your spouse sit down and discuss your values, thoughts, ideas with the requests being made of you and come up with a solution that works for your family.

Don't forget that respect and sensitivity are just as important to living with dignity as is speaking honestly.

Remember the Indians in *Dances with Wolves*, for whom confrontations were always resolved in a way that allowed all parties to retain their dignity?

Surround yourself with people who welcome authentic conversations.

Recognize the people in your life who can't handle authentic conversations. It will be up to you where they fit in your life. Sometimes we have people who can't handle authentic conversations and we must keep them in our lives e.g. family, teachers/coaches, bosses etc. Set boundaries, set up the situations for success e.g. have buffers, interact around safe structured activities, and recognize these can be difficult situations. One wise client who had become quite competent at having authentic conversations also had many challenging family gatherings, which she could not resolve with authenticity. She finally realized she would have to just love her family, take care of herself during the get togethers and vent when they were over.

Homework

Now that you have been working towards warriorhood, what are you finding out about yourself?

What do you notice about where you have been and where you are going?

Is there anything different about your mindset?

Has your body changed?

Have you noticed a surge of energy when you say No to whom or whatever won't support you, and Yes to taking a stand?

Journal your thoughts, your new practices, your reactions, what you are learning, and what is different in your body.

One way to assist you on the path of authentic living is to write standards for yourself:

Do you want people around you who can speak the truth or are you still comfortable with elephants on the table, burping, farting and throwing up?

Do you want people close to you who don't keep their agreements?

Do you want people close to you who don't call you back?

Do you want people close to you who only want you to agree with them?

Do you want people close to you who "brainwash" and "use" you for their insecure self-serving needs?

Do you want people close to you who steamroll you and your opinions?

Do you want people close to you who never question you?

Do you want people close to you who never ask you about you?

Do you want people close to you who only tell you what you want to hear?

Think about our heroes: the Liberian women, the Afghan Olympian, the young girls in Afghanistan pursuing their education in spite of having acid thrown on their faces.

They have set standards for themselves for which they are willing to risk their lives.

In 2002, three American heroes of mine risked not their lives, but certainly their way of life, in order to stand up for what they believed.

2. Coleen Rowley, FBI

3. Sherron Walkiuns, Enron

4. Cynthia Cooper, World.com

Each had the courage to go against the tide and say enough is enough.

Kudos to *Time* magazine for making them 2002's *Persons of the Year*. What these women said was not popular, nor well received. *Time* recognized them for their integrity.

On a scale of 1-10, these women are a 10. Where do you put yourself? Where do you want to be? Let's get going!

Endnotes

---

[i] Timothy J. Galpin and Mark Herndon, *The Complete Guide to Mergers and Acquisitions: Process Tools to Support M@A Integration at Every Level* (San Francisco: Jossey-Bass, 2000), 93-95.

[ii] Karola Alford, "Gender Culture in a Relationship Workshop for College Students," *Journal of College Counseling* 4 No. 1 (2001): 85.

[iii] *The Miracle Worker,* Arthur Penn. Playfilm Productions, 1962.

[iv] *Ray,* Taylor Hackford, Bristol Bay Productions, 2004.

Chapter Five

Compassion for Missed Opportunity

While writing this book I actually sat in a car with the motor running while the driver filled it up with gas because I couldn't think of the request I wanted to make: (Should I just leap over the seat and turn off the motor, should I jump out of the car and say what, should I open the window and ask that the motor be turned off?) Game over: the driver was back in the car and the gas tank was filled and we were on our way. I did not bring up my concern for the next 30 minutes we were driving. No success but lots of learning.

Hang on in the Bumps

Remember the little girl whose Mom said if she made a request of her Dad he would hit her, well not all requests have that horrible outcome and they also may not be met with open arms.

One client made a request of a service man whose response was to yell at her.

A parent I know made a totally appropriate request of her teenage daughter whose response was to start hysterically yelling at her.

A spouse's request of his wife to kiss hello and goodbye and to have conversations in the evening while they were together was met with, "you want so much from me, I can never do enough for you, you are so demanding."

A spouse's request of her husband that he plan his vacation with the guys in a way that would be best for the family was met with, "why do you always do this to me?"

These irrational responses are just that irrational. All of the requests were appropriate, reasonable and doable. Don't stop making requests because of others irrational responses. You have the right to make requests!

The same can be true for declining and having authentic conversations. You are not always going to get rational responses. Begin to weed out the people who can't play at the emotionally healthy level you want to play at. Don't give emotionally unhealthy behavior power to keep you stuck!

Remember the Success Stories

Do I really want to go through this, you ask yourself and why? Remember our first chapter on why it is so important to have tools for self-advocacy.

The world is a more complicated place to live. Just having one tool called "people-pleasing" is not enough.

There are different levels of becoming a warrior. First and foremost is your own personal world. Cleaning out your resentment drawer is the first line of business. Take a look at the domain of finances. Are there areas where you can stop the money from going out and request more money to come in? Remember our young woman who almost doubled her salary by one request conversation. How about the women in the marriages who now have more financial autonomy!

Move next to the domain of love. If you are single there are lots of great books to read e.g. Steve Harvey, *Act Like a Lady, Think Like a Man,* and Greg Behrendt and Liz Tuccillo's *He's Just Not That Into You.*

Most of them are asking you to develop STANDARDS for yourself. It is time! If we women require our men to be the best they can be, everyone wins!

Take a look at resentments you might have with your family. I recommend attending a Family of Origin Workshop (Resources) to understand your history with your family. Understand and make friends with your past. Find your voice for your life today! Remember Julie's words to her Mom, "Mom you have courage. You are strong. You think something you say it."

Make requests of your children. Say No to being taken advantage of. Remember our Mom who with one request took laundry and shopping off of her plate. Remember how proud her children were of contributing to the family. Allow your children the joy of being part of the family's success.

Hopefully you are not in an abusive relationship but if you are, please say No to the abuse. The only appropriate response from the abuser to a 911 call made by the person being abused is "Thank You, I might have really hurt you. Thank you for stopping me." One young couple is healing together because the abuser said, "Thank you for getting me help before it was too late." Remember the ONLY appropriate response from the abuser if you call 911 to report the abuse is "Thank You"!

Find balance in your life. Say No to martyr, victim, and overworking! Say Yes to healthy eating, exercise, grounding practices, anything that supports you living in joy, love, peace, courage, contentment, and passion for openers.

It is up to you the level warrior you want to become. Start with your own personal world and live in it resentment free. If you have a passion/cause that gets your juices going move on out into the world where there are lots of warriors taking a stand against the darkness in the world.

Frolic or Struggle?

Balancing between new behavior and old behavior can be like entering the surf. I remember one particular day in Lanai getting in the water was like being tossed around in life. If you tried to muscle your way, determined to stand your ground you were either dumped, unceremoniously onto the beach by large incoming waves or dragged out into the ocean under the water by a strong outgoing wave.

Everyone played in the waves in different ways. One young child jumped up and hit the wave with his backside. One young couple clung together letting the waves toss them around. Some people dove through the waves, some dove under the waves, and some dove up and over the waves. One woman who swam into shore from about a half a mile out was an inspiration to watch. She kept her head, with snorkel on, down and just kept swimming "by feel". When she felt she was swimming forward and going backward she didn't panic she just patiently waited for the next wave and began swimming with the wave toward the beach. There are times we all need to wait patiently when we find ourselves going against the flow of life until we can go with the flow of life.

In addition, if you trusted the process of floating over the incoming waves allowing the strong outgoing waves to carry you out to the calm ocean beyond, it all worked perfectly. The same was true of riding the flow back onto the beach. At one moment, feeling myself so close to the beach and yet still not feeling any ground under me, I panicked, almost going into the muscling process. No, No, No all is well, "trust" a voice said, back into the flow of the ocean to be gently dropped onto the beach. I did and it did!

The same day a school of spinner dolphins hung out all day in the water with us. Their playful frolicking served as a reminder of how we can choose to play in life. Do you want to effort and struggle or dance and frolic? It is up to you!

Bibliography

1. Alford, Karola "Gender Culture in a Relationship Workshop for College Students." *Journal of College Counseling* 4 No. 1 (2001): 85.

2. Allcorn, Seth. *Codependency in the Workplace: A Guide for Employee Assistance and Human Resource Professionals.* New York: Quorum Books, 1992.

3. Braiker, Ph.D Harriet B. *The Disease to Please.* U.S.A.: McGraw Hill, 2001.

4. Brant, Renee. "Case Vignette: Child Abuse or Acceptable Cultural Norms." *Ethics @ Behavior* 5 No. 3 (1995): 283.

5. Cahill, Ann J. *Rethinking Rape.* New York: Cornell University Press, 2001.

6. Callaway, Allison. *Deaf Children in China.* Washington D.C.: Gallaudit University Press, 2000.

7. *Dances with Wolves,* Kevin Costner. Tig Productions, 1990.

8. Davis, Kimberly. "Making Blended Families Work," *Ebony* 55, No. 12 (October 2000): 40.

9. Escher, Ursula. *Self–Defense for Kids.* Korea: Pak's Karate Studio, 2003.

10. Feltham, Colin and Windy Dryden. *Brief Counseling: A Practical, Integrative Approach.* England: Open University Press, 2006.

11. *Forrest Gump*, Robert Zemeckis. Paramount Pictures, 1994.

12. Galpin, Timothy J. and Mark Herndon. *The Complete Guide to Mergers and Acquisitions: Process Tools to Support M@A Integration at Every Level.* San Francisco: Jossey-Bass, 2000.

13. Gladwell, Malcolm. *The Tipping Point.* New York: Little Brown and Company, 2000, 2001.

14. Konzak, Burt PhD, and Melina and Sonya Konzak. Girl *Power.* Canada: Sports Book Publisher, 1999.

15. Lamar, Donna F. *Transcending Turmoil: Survivors of Dysfunctional Families.* New York: Plenum Press, 1992.

16. La Torre, Mary Anne. " Meditation and Psychotherapy: An Effective Combination." *Perspectives in Psychiatric Care* 37 (2001): 1.

17. Levinson, Harry. *The Great Jackass Fallacy.* Cambridge: Harvard University Press, 1973.

18. Lewis, Michael. "The Man Who Crashed the World," *Vanity Fair* (August 2009): 98.

19. "McGraw's Search for his Father," *The Week* (November 13, 2009): 10.

20. Miller, John P. *The Contemplative Practitioner: Meditation in Education and the Professions.* Connecticut: Bergin @ Garvey, 1994.

21. Mitroff, Ian I. *Managing Crises before They Happen: What Every Executive and Manager Needs to Know about Crisis Management.* New York: Amacon, 2001.

22. Norment, Lynn. "What's Behind the Dramatic Rise in Rapes?" *Ebony* 44, no. 11 (September 1991): 92.

23. Peled, Einat, Zvi Eisikovits, Guy Enosh, and Zeev Winstok. "Choice and Empowerment for Battered Women Who Stay: Toward a Constructivist Model." *Social Work* 45, No. 1 (2000): 9.

24. Pickering W.S.F. and Geoffrey Walford. *Durkheim's Suicide: A Century of Research and Debate*. United Kingdom: Routledge 2000.

25. *Pray the Devil Back To Hell,* Abigail E. Disney and Gini Reticker. Fork Films, 2008.

26. Raines, Clare and Lara Ewing. *The Art of Connecting: How to Overcome Differences, Build Rapport, and Communicate Effectively with Anyone*. New York: Amacon, 2006.

27. Radford, Benjamin. "Predator Panic: a Closer Look," *Skeptical Inquirer* 30, (September 2006): 1.

28. *Ray,* Taylor Hackford. Bristol Bay Productions, 2004.

29. Robinson, Duke. *Too Nice for Your Own Good*. New York: Warner Books, 1997.

30. Rubin, Harriet. "The Power of Words" *Fast Company*, January 1999. http://www.fastcompany.com/magazine/21/flores.html.

31. Sanderson, Christiane. *Counseling Adult Servivors of Child Sexual Abuse*. London: Jessica Kingsley, 2006.

32. Searle, John R. *Speech Acts: An Essay in the Philosophy of Language*. Cambridge, Cambridge University Press, 1969.

33. Skowron, Elizabeth A., Stephen R. Wester, and Razia Azen. "Differentiation of Self mediates College Stress and Adjustment." *Journal of Counseling and Development* 84, No.1 (2004): 69.

34. Smith, Ph.D. Manual J. *When I say No, I Feel Guilty*. United States, Canada: Bantam Books, 1975.

35. *South Park,* Trey Parker and Matt Stone. Comedy Central, 1997-2010.

36.   Strauss, Kandra. "Dumping the Stress by Getting Fit," *National Education Association* 20, No. 7 (April 2002): 35.

37.   Talking Heads. *Once in a Lifetime on Remain in Light* (audio cd). Burbank, California: Distributed by Warner Brothers/ Wea, 1980.

38.   *The Miracle Worker,* Arthur Penn. Playfilm Productions, 1962.

39.   "Verbatim." *Time,* February 2, 2009, 20.

40.   Wallerstein, Judith S. and Joan B. Kelly. *Surviving the Breakup: How Children and Parents Cope with Divorce.* New York: Basic Books, 1966.

41. Winkler, Karen. "Kinsey Sex Research, and the Body of Knowledge: Let's Talk about Sex." *Women's Studies Quarterly* 33, No. ¾, (2005): 285.

42.   Zusne, Leonard, and Warren H. Jones. *Anomalistic Psychology: A Study of Magical Thinking.* New Jersey: Lawrence Erlbaum Associates, 1989.

Resources

1. Breakthrough at Caron, 1-800-268-6259, www.breakthroughatcaron.org

2. The Hoffman Process, 1-800-506-5253, www.hoffmaninstitute.org

3. The Meadows, Survivors I, 1-800-632-3697, www.themeadows.com

4. Onsite, Living Centered Program, 1-800-341-7432, www.onsiteworkshops.com

5. www.developingyourbackbone.com

6. To order books: www.createspace.com/3481370

6567683R0

Made in the USA
Charleston, SC
08 November 2010